Beyond the Rainbow

PRAISE FOR *BEYOND THE RAINBOW*

Profound grief has the potential either to close us down or break us open. As much as anyone I know, Beth Knopik chooses the latter path. In this fearless account of her daughter's unexpected death, the author insists that there is blessing to be wrestled even from the most searing loss. Leanna Mae's death forced a reckoning; in its wake the author discovered a deeper connection to her God, her daughter, and her community. Beth Knopik's account invites readers to discover the life to be found on the other side of loss.

The Reverend Margaret LaMotte Torrence

How can a mother go forward in her life when confronted with the unthinkable, the death of her child? Beyond the Rainbow *is a heart-rending, heart-healing answer to this question, the story of a mother's grief and her surrender to the transforming power of grace. A beautifully written and profoundly moving book.*

David Zapata;
entrepreneur, poet, writer, editor

With powerful imagery, Beyond the Rainbow *describes the entire process of how Beth Knopik and her family came through tragic loss and discovered God's grace. This memoir will be a gift to many readers who are experiencing grief and seeking answers. Beautiful and moving, it shines on every page.*

Betsy Rapoport;
author, writer, editor, master life coach

Beyond the Rainbow is Beth Knopik's personal and riveting story of her journey through heartbreak and hopelessness to true healing. Her tale is a must-read, not only for those finding their way through insurmountable grief, but for anyone seeking profound and valuable lessons in Faith, Hope and Love. This book is an honest, touching and beautiful tribute from a mother to her daughter, and a gift to all who read it.

Con Nicholas;
retired high school English educator, poet

Beyond the Rainbow is a must-read for anyone coping with the loss of a loved one. Compelling and moving, honest and genuine, the book offers an intimate look into the experience of a family facing incredible tragedy. Somehow, though, the lasting lesson is uplifting and empowering, and the wisdoms offered can impart new insight into the terrible inevitability of loss.

Rebecca Abrahamson;
journalist and writing educator

Beyond
the
Rainbow

A Mother's Journey
Through Grief to Grace

Beth Knopik

NASHVILLE
NEW YORK • LONDON • MELBOURNE • VANCOUVER

Beyond the Rainbow

A Mother's Journey Through Grief to Grace

Published in New York, New York, by Morgan James Publishing. Morgan James is a trademark of Morgan James, LLC. www.MorganJamesPublishing.com

Proudly distributed by Ingram Publisher Services.

Scripture taken from INTERNATIONAL STANDARD VERSION, copyright© 1996–2008 by the ISV Foundation. All rights reserved internationally.

The stories in this book reflect the author's recollection of events. Some names have been changed to protect the privacy of those depicted. Dialogue has been re-created from memory.

Morgan James BOGO™

A **FREE** ebook edition is available for you or a friend with the purchase of this print book.

[ ]

CLEARLY SIGN YOUR NAME ABOVE

Instructions to claim your free ebook edition:
1. Visit MorganJamesBOGO.com
2. Sign your name CLEARLY in the space above
3. Complete the form and submit a photo of this entire page
4. You or your friend can download the ebook to your preferred device

ISBN 9781631958816 paperback
ISBN 9781631958823 ebook
Library of Congress Control Number:
2022931241

Cover Design by:
Megan Dillon
megan@creativeninjadesigns.com

Interior Design by:
Christopher Kirk
www.GFSstudio.com

Cover photo by:
Michael Klauber
@ Victoria Falls, Zimbabwe, 2011

Photos of Leanna Knopik and Beth Knopik by:
Andrea Hillebrand

Morgan James PUBLISHING

Builds with... **Habitat for Humanity** Peninsula and Greater Williamsburg

Morgan James is a proud partner of Habitat for Humanity Peninsula and Greater Williamsburg. Partners in building since 2006.

Get involved today! Visit MorganJamesPublishing.com/giving-back

This book is dedicated to Steve and Rogers, the loves of my life.

*In memory of The Reverend Dr. H. Ray Woody
and Dr. Gregory Simmons.*

"I am a little pencil in the hand of a writing God who is sending a love letter to the world."
Mother Teresa

Honoring the life and legacy of Leanna Mae Knopik

Table of Contents

Acknowledgments

This book could not have been written without God's help and hard work from different people. I owe an enormous debt of gratitude to those who played a part in bringing it to fruition.

Many thanks to my editors, Kelly Madrone and Andrew Szanton, for your steadfast encouragement and for helping me to put my thoughts and heart on paper.

For granting interviews, I want to thank Carolyn Moore, Clay Thomas, Caryn Young, Christina Astore, and Joey Schwab.

For reading the book, or sections of the book in draft form, and offering helpful additions, suggestions, and corrections, I want to thank Ann Spangler, Betsy Rapoport, Steve Knopik, Rebecca Abrahamson, Callie Chappell-Nicholas, Con Nicholas, and David Zapata.

The writings of James Tyrrell were also helpful to the scenes I wrote about South Africa.

To Tom Dean, my agent and now friend, I am grateful for your belief in my story along with your guidance and support. And thank you to Morgan James Publishing for taking my book the last mile to bookstores far and wide.

And finally, for love and support day in and day out, I want to thank my husband, Steve Knopik, and our son, Rogers Knopik. You are the true loves of my life.

Introduction

S ometimes, a storm begins quietly, with a few drops of rain before the downpour.

For me, it all started with a question.

A proud and devoted mother of two school-aged kids, I sometimes felt that my life wasn't serving a higher purpose. I was in the world, grateful for my life and my family, but not fully satisfied. During quiet moments, I found myself asking God, "What's next?" or "Why am I here? *Please show me.*"

I now know that the answer to that question is bigger than my brain, yet there are pieces I can grasp and hold close. More than anything, I have learned to look *beyond* what is—or at least what seems to be—to find the deeper meaning.

The mere idea of a parent losing a child is so painful that to contemplate it is something we avoid at all costs. To live it is to be dragged through devastation so gaping that it feels cruelly cavernous. I understand, and it is true—losing a child leaves a hole that can never be repaired. Yet what I have learned is that it can be filled.

In her brief sixteen years on this earth, my daughter Leanna gave me many gifts in the form of life lessons. Some of her greatest gifts, however, have been since her passing. Leanna taught me that when you are truly called to do something, you cannot ignore it. I have also learned that God's plan for us is way bigger than we can possibly imagine.

When the summer of 2012 began, I had no idea that a storm was coming. My teens were setting off for summer camps hundreds of miles from home: Leanna to a Christian work camp in West Virginia, and her younger brother, Rogers, to a performing arts camp in New York.

The year before, Leanna, along with her work crew in West Virginia, repaired and improved homes for struggling families. She learned to use power drills, electric saws, and industrial staple guns, but most of all, she soaked in the deep fulfillment that comes from serving others. Leanna had fun, too, as her crew leader, Matt, later described in letters and conversations. He told me about a playful paint fight, which explained Leanna's speckled sneakers. Then there was the afternoon when, though exhausted from a long day building and painting a set of stairs outside a trailer home, Matt spied a freshly mowed field strewn with clumps of just-cut grass. Only half-joking, he asked if anyone wanted to join him in running through the clippings. The hard work and humidity left them tired, drenched, and sluggish. Still, Leanna didn't hesitate. Eyes twinkling and wearing a wide grin, she hopped up in a heartbeat. Squealing and laughing, she and Matt darted across the field, scooping up handfuls of moist grass and hurling them at one another. Matt's story didn't surprise me; that was just Leanna. She lived without hesitation. To laugh, to help, to love.

———

Two days before Leanna left for camp in 2012, she met Christina, one of her best friends, for a farewell lunch.

"I'm so excited for you!" Christina exclaimed. "You've been talking nonstop about this trip since the day you got back last year."

Yet, as she studied her friend across the table, Christina was also concerned; Leanna didn't look quite right. She was as pretty as ever, but something was slightly off. Her body was a shade thinner, her mood a bit off, as Christina would later describe. It was a difference subtle enough that only a close friend would notice.

Although she hesitated to bring up a sore subject, Christina felt compelled.

"Are you still having those chest pains?" Christina asked, trying to sound casual.

"I'm okay," Leanna replied to her friend's troubled face. "Really. Please, don't worry," Leanna implored.

"It was almost as if Leanna knew something she chose not to reveal," Christina told me later. This was not the first time Christina had wondered if Leanna had a special knowing she kept to herself. Maybe it wasn't conscious—but perhaps a secret in Leanna's soul.

As they finished their lunch, Christina fidgeted with the napkin in her lap. Whatever it was that nagged her, she dreaded parting with Leanna. Christina was about to start summer school for college prep, and her best friend was heading off to West Virginia. Despite her reassurances—even while sitting right there in front of Christina—for some reason, Leanna already felt remote.

The heat rose in waves off the pavement as the girls crossed the parking lot. The sound of flip-flops clapping against their heels stopped suddenly as Leanna spun around to face her friend. "Don't be sad. This isn't forever. . .We get to see each other in two short weeks for the Coldplay concert!" She threw her arms around Christina, pulling her close.

"Yeeessss, of course, it's going to be the best ever! I can't wait!" Christina squealed. Then, head tilted, she stepped back and took in Leanna's quirky smile.

I'm overthinking things, Christina thought. *Everything's alright. Besides, I'll see her in two weeks.*

"I love you, Leanna. Have fun in West Virginia. I'll count the days until I see you again!"

"I love you, too, Tina," Leanna grinned, giving her friend another quick hug before they climbed into their cars.

———

Leanna was so eager for her mission trip that a week before leaving, she was already stuffing shorts and t-shirts into her duffel bag. Yet in the midst of her preparations, after her lunch with Christina, she confessed to me that something was wrong.

"Mom? I don't feel very good."

I looked up from my computer. Leanna's face was pale.

"My chest hurts when I climb the stairs, and I have a hard time catching my breath. It's like there's pressure on my chest."

At sixteen years old, Leanna was vibrant and athletic. She carried a full load of advanced courses at school, rowed six days a week for Sarasota Crew, and had earned a black belt in taekwondo. Like most kids, she had her share of sniffles and coughs growing up, but nothing remarkable.

"Okay, sweetheart," I told her. "Let's go see the doctor, just in case."

I was not surprised Leanna was feeling worn out. Between athletics and her busy social life and now getting ready to leave for camp, she was always at full tilt.

In the meantime, Rogers ventured off to Hancock, New York, leaving a week before Leanna. On the morning of his departure, he was up well before sunrise. He and a friend had a flight to catch from Tampa to Newark where they would board a bus for the four-hour drive from Newark to Hancock. We were just getting his things together, making sure he hadn't forgotten his rain jacket, when Leanna surprised us all by appearing at the top of the stairs wearing her favorite flannel pants and a t-shirt. Bleary-eyed, she descended, and the two of them shared a hug. None of us dreamed it would be their last.

Leanna's pediatrician smiled at me as he looped the stethoscope around his neck. "It's just a virus that's going around," he proclaimed. "Nothing spooky."

My shoulders relaxed as I released a breath I didn't know I was holding. "Leanna really wants to leave for camp tomorrow," I said. "Would that be okay?"

"As long as she gets as much rest as possible and drinks a lot of fluids, yes, it's okay," he reassured us.

Just a virus, I repeated to myself. *Nothing spooky.*

"Are you sure you shouldn't be resting right now?" I watched Leanna as she hunched over an electric pink t-shirt laid out on the laundry room counter.

"I'm okay, Mom," she said, clutching a little white bottle of puff paint. "I need to get this done so it can dry before tomorrow."

"What are you doing, anyway?"

"I'm writing out this Bible verse." She paused and squinted at her handiwork. "It's Romans 12:2—the theme of the week at work camp. I'm gonna wear it during our worship services."

I joined her at the counter, peering over her shoulder. She'd taken a piece of cardboard and written the verse on it in painstakingly perfect script, then tucked the cardboard under the shirt to use as a guide. I read the words aloud. "'Do not be conformed to this world but continually be transformed by the renewal of your minds so that you will be able to determine what God's will is—what is proper, praising and perfect.' That's beautiful."

Leanna nodded. She didn't look up, but I could feel her smiling back at me.

The next morning, Leanna traipsed downstairs in well-worn jeans and a flannel shirt, a backpack hanging from her shoulder, her blonde hair wound into a cockeyed, messy bun. "I'm ready!" she exclaimed.

My husband Steve tossed Leanna's duffel into the trunk of the car. We piled in and drove to the bus, just five minutes away. Already there waiting for us were teens and adults from a church in Cape Coral, ninety minutes south of Sarasota. When Leanna had first heard about the camp two years before, something about it had captured her attention. It didn't matter that the trip was sponsored by another church with people she didn't know; she wanted to be part of it. "Those families up there need help," she had said. "I really want to go."

When she had returned from West Virginia the previous summer, the bus stopped at a Cracker Barrel along the highway to drop her off. As she climbed down the stairs, what seemed like the entire busload of kids followed her. It had only been a week, but they were laughing, crying, hugging—then more hugging—as if they had known each other forever. I knew from my own experience participating in church projects and charity fundraisers that when people are in service together, instant bonds are formed. But that fast, easy friendship was also just Leanna's way. It was clear that in only one week, something had clicked for her. Leanna grew even more excited about opportunities to help others and was especially eager to go back.

Steve pulled into a parking space, and we all climbed out. I hugged my daughter tight while Steve retrieved her bag and loaded it on the bus. "Keep me posted on how you're feeling," I instructed, locking eyes with her.

"Okay, Mamma," she said. "I'll be fine."

When Steve returned, Leanna stood on her tiptoes and wrapped her arms around his neck. "Happy early Father's Day! I'm sorry Rogers and I won't be here to celebrate with you tomorrow," she pouted.

"It's okay. The work you're doing is very important," Steve assured her. "I love you, girl. Feel better!"

As Leanna turned and walked toward the bus, Steve and I settled back into the car. He started the ignition, but before he could back out, I stopped him. "Let's wait a minute," I said. We watched her disappear into the bus, and through the window, I saw her blonde bun bounce and then slide out of view when she took a seat with the others. My stomach churned, roiling with an unease I sometimes felt when my kids left home. But I told myself that was normal; Leanna was where she needed to be. She was showing her independence and doing something good for the world. I couldn't stand in her way.

As the bus retreated, Leanna peered back at us through the tinted window, flashing that sweet, silly smile as she waved goodbye.

In the first ten hours or so after she left, I texted Leanna a handful of times. Twenty-four hours after leaving home, she still felt weak and nauseated, and she wasn't eating. I urged her to try bland foods like crackers and drink fluids.

I'll try, she responded.

On Monday afternoon, just two days later, she wrote, *I don't know what to do, Mom—whether to come home or not.*

I didn't know, either. I wanted Leanna back with me, where I could care for her, but I told myself not to overreact.

Pray about it, Leanna, I wrote. Decisions should be made with a clear mind, I reasoned, and prayers were the best way I knew at the time to find clarity.

My relationship to prayer was a longstanding commitment. In my early years, when the broken home of my childhood made me feel adrift, prayer reliably served as a compass. Church had provided the structure I needed to cope, and prayer oriented me toward an answer. My faith was not solely pinned to the church—I often connected with God in the nature that surrounded me in my Virginia upbringing. Still, prayer soothed, guided, and pointed to answers. When in doubt, pray.

Yet by Monday evening, Leanna was vomiting, and at that point, it was obvious to me—she couldn't stay there. I urged her to tell the group leaders that she needed to pack up and leave, but even then, I left the decision up to her. A few hours later she texted.

I have to come home.

Her plane ticket was waiting.

Someone else will have to bring home my bag, she added. *I won't be able to carry it.*

Alarms went off inside me. *Why not?* I responded, gripping my phone, trying to hold on to any last bit of calm I could.

I'm just too weak.

Tears filled my eyes. My girl would be flying home *alone* in such a delicate state that she couldn't manage her bag. Steve finally admitted the depth of his concern.

"But she'll be home soon, and then we'll get this taken care of," he declared. He was right. Everything would be okay. After all, kids get sick all the time, and her doctor had reassured us. Once she was home, she'd be fine.

———

My fingers turned pale as I clutched the steering wheel. I took a steadying breath and resisted the urge to accelerate. Josh, Leanna's boyfriend, and I were driving to Tampa International Airport to retrieve Leanna.

Once there, we paced in the arrivals area, Josh anxiously combing his fingers through his ginger hair. Then my fear spiked to panic as I saw an airline employee approaching, pushing a wheelchair. In the chair sat my daughter, her boundless energy apparently leaked out of her. I attempted a casual smile, trying to conceal my anxiety. From there, Josh and I wheeled the chair to the car and helped my daughter, normally athletic and exuberant, settle into the back seat.

We drove back to Sarasota, the car silent most of the way. It was clear Leanna was exhausted, and now that she was back with me, I just wanted her to rest after first seeing the doctor. Josh sat next to her in the backseat, studying her intently—the fear clear in his eyes—and holding her hand.

———

The young blonde nurse at the pediatrician's office crinkled her nose then shook her head slightly. She seemed competent, yet she could not get a read on Leanna's blood pressure. With a bewildered look on her face, she tried again. Then again. No luck.

"She must be badly dehydrated," the doctor surmised as he reviewed her vital signs. "You need to take her right away to the emergency room at Sarasota Memorial Hospital." Gone was the relaxed smile of our earlier visit. "Nothing spooky" had turned into an urgent order.

Twenty minutes later, we arrived at the hospital—the same twelve-story white stucco building where Leanna had come into the world sixteen years before. We stepped into the building where my children had been born, surrounded by the walls that witnessed the first breath of their lives.

The nurses who examined Leanna moved with purpose. Leanna's skin was hot to the touch. She had a virus and was dehydrated. Still, they assured me that a few days' rest and IV hydration would have her back to normal. *Vitamins and nutrients*, I told myself. *All Leanna needs are fluids and some time to let the virus run its course.*

Yet, even with all the fluids that they pumped into her, Leanna's pulse, blood pressure, and breathing remained labored. She squirmed in her hospital bed, unable to get comfortable. After nearly thirty minutes of measuring and monitoring, the nurses realized her heartbeat was still unstable. They shifted to a higher gear.

More doctors arrived, each with their own theory. Over and over, the nurses checked the monitors. They didn't say much to me. They didn't have to; their expressions conveyed everything.

I fumbled in my purse. Pulling out my phone, I dialed Steve. "You need to come over here!"

Steve arrived just in time to hear the doctors say, "Your daughter needs to go to All Children's Hospital in St. Petersburg. You can ride with her in the ambulance."

Steve glanced at me, his alarmed expression imploring, *What did I just walk into?*

Moments later, a nurse hustled in. "Change of plans—they're taking Leanna by helicopter." Steve and I looked at one other, panicked.

Within minutes, two men and a woman wearing dark-gray jump-suits appeared, their movements focused and fast like action heroes in a movie. As they strapped Leanna to a gurney, I leaned over my daughter. "Dad and I will be right behind you, sweetheart," I assured her. "We'll see you at the children's hospital."

A trace of fear flashed in Leanna's eyes as she nodded back at me. "Okay, Mamma."

With efficient urgency, the Bayflite team closed around Leanna and wheeled her gurney down the hall. They disappeared into the elevator and ascended to the roof.

I turned to Steve, my mind spinning. "Why are they airlifting her? It's just a precaution, right? They're just playing it safe." Even as the words poured from my lips, I heard myself fumbling to reassure myself.

As was typical, his facial expression revealed nothing indicating his inner workings. "I hope you're right," he said flatly. "Let's go."

Driving out of the parking garage at 11:00 p.m., Steve and I glanced upward and saw the blinking light of Leanna's helicopter rise from the roof followed by the *whup-whup-whup* of the chopper blades. Our daughter was flying into the black with strangers we were forced to trust.

We followed the blinking light along the roads as far as we could, then lost sight of it in the dark.

PART
ONE

Chapter 1

I've always escaped, whenever I could, to the water and the woods. To be at my best, centered and close to God, I need to be in nature. I feel a soul connection with every plant and animal, with the air itself and the infinite sky. When I am surrounded by magnificent old trees, I connect with a deep part of myself and seem to trust the path before me without worrying—without even thinking. Being in nature for me is just that: *being*. Time does not seem to exist. The wind, the waves, the trees, the grass, and the animals make no demands and have no expectations. My mind can surrender to my heart. The sound of rain falling on dry leaves brings on euphoria because I know that I am a part of it all, a tiny piece of creation, and I do not have to do anything, only *be*.

On the morning of my routine prenatal check-up, I woke to the sound of gentle waves rolling in. After moving from Virginia to Florida, the Gulf of Mexico had become my escape. As often as I could, I walked along its edges, finding peace in the rhythm of the warm water rolling in and out. At sixteen weeks pregnant and with a doctor's visit that day, I yearned for a mindful moment to thank God for the life growing inside me. A walk by the water was calling.

I rose from my bed as the big orange sun crested the horizon. I threw on a t-shirt and shorts, grabbed my flip-flops, and took the elevator to the ground level. A crowd of crows cawed in the distance as I passed from the cool conditioned air into the warm breeze. I meandered through the condominium's maze of security gates and the pool area, each gate closing behind me. I slipped onto the beach and sighed into the familiar feeling of fine sand as it massaged the soles of my feet. Crossing the wide expanse of Siesta Key's beach, I reached the hard-packed surface along the fringe of the water, my heart beating faster now. After years of running on this same shore, trying to raise my heart rate, it now took little effort for me to feel winded. With my new reality, I had to slow my pace. I was going to be a mother in the fall, and I was already so in love with my child.

As I looked out at the rippling water, my mind traveled back to my youth, when the waters of the Atlantic off the shores of Virginia Beach lured me with their playful waves. I'd fix my eyes upon the surface, which whipped and frothed near my younger self's toes, and imagined the life I would come to live.

Even then, the water seemed to hold answers for me. It listened as I lamented the breakup from my first real boyfriend. It held hope when I visited it with my heart heavy from sporadic spats with my mom.

Later, as I contemplated my career and worked hard to achieve success in finance, waves worked wonders on my restless mind. Somehow, they knew what I didn't in my youth—the business world of banking wasn't the life I was destined to follow.

Here, with my belly full of a precious baby, I marveled at what had happened in just a few short years—moving to Florida, starting a new job, meeting the love of my life. . . the changes were profound. The tame waters of the Gulf of Mexico were a calmer and more peaceful version of the tumultuous waves of the Atlantic, and they soothed my heart that was so full of anticipation. I couldn't wait to meet our new baby, and the water reminded me that all good things come in time. *Thank you, God, for this precious being. I promise I will be the best mom I can be.*

A gentle breeze carried the smell of seawater, and I took a deep breath. The path before me was filled with love and adventure. I was blessed.

A seagull's cry roused me from this repose. Tummy rumbling, I traipsed back to the condo. Every morning before work, Steve prepared a bowl of fresh fruit for me. Washing and cutting every piece with care was one of his ways of supporting our new little life. Famished, I popped a piece of bread into the toaster oven then grabbed my bottle of prenatal vitamins and poured a glass of water. I sat down to breakfast thinking about the day ahead. I would shower, find something that fit over my expanding waistline, then drive to the doctor's office just ten minutes away. I could not wait to hear the baby's heartbeat again.

———

"A little cold here. Sorry, Beth." I winced as Dr. Sandler squeezed the clear goop onto my abdomen then began to roll the ultrasound wand across it. Leaning back, I closed my eyes and tried to relax, yet the question in my head was persistent. *Is this normal? Doesn't the technician do the ultrasound and just give the results to the obstetrician? Why had she summoned Dr. Sandler?*

"Okay, let's take a look," Dr. Sandler said as he squinted at the monitor. I opened my eyes and tried for a moment to read his face. Nothing. He rolled the wand left then right. Up then down. Finally, he nodded and sat back. "Beth," he said softly, "I'd like to have my colleague, Dr. Daley, take a look."

Two words escaped my tightening throat. "What's wrong?"

"Why don't you get dressed, and we'll talk in my office." His tone was solemn.

A few minutes later, I sat across from Dr. Sandler, fighting waves of nausea and fear. "Beth, I am concerned with the baby's development. We've already called Dr. Daley's office just a few floors down from here. He is a maternal-fetal medicine specialist. He'll see you right away. I know this is alarming, but I don't want to get into conjecture until we're sure of what we're looking at. Kelly's going to walk you down there."

I nodded, swallowing hard. Earlier this morning, everything was perfect.

I went to stand, but my legs were weak, and I fell back in the chair for a moment. Finally, I rose. Dr. Sandler's nurse was standing in the doorway. "Hi, Beth," she said. Her head was tilted, and her mouth was set in that almost-smile that's meant to convey sympathy.

Suddenly, everyone was extra nice, talking to me so gently as if too much noise would shatter me. Maybe it would have.

Three floors down, I lay there in my gown, hands by my side, as Dr. Daley reached for the tube of clear jelly. I watched his face assume the same expressionless stare Dr. Sandler had worn as he took in whatever he saw. He replaced the wand in its holder. The nurse wiped the gel from my belly and pulled up the crisp white blanket to cover me, tucking it a bit at the edges as if I was a child.

I reached down and rested my palms on my abdomen. *Please*, I begged. *Please*.

Dr. Daley stood, rolled his stool over, then sat back down, placing a hand on the table next to me. When he finally spoke, it was as if his words floated in from somewhere else. I saw his lips moving, but his voice came to me in pieces. He echoed Dr. Sandler. "Abnormalities . . . not developing properly . . ."

I wanted to question him. To protest. But looking in Dr. Daley's eyes, the message was clear.

"Beth," his hand moved to my arm, where it rested softly for a moment. "I'm so sorry to give you this news."

A few minutes later, I found myself back in Dr. Daley's reception area where Kelly was waiting for me, then I was back up in Dr. Sandler's office with the phone receiver in my hand.

One ring. Two.

"Hello?"

"Steve?"

"Hey, Beth. How was—"

"Steve, I'm at Dr. Sandler's office. You . . . you need to come down here," I heard myself stuttering. Everything else inside me had shut down as if my body was channeling what little energy I had just to keep me going.

"Beth, what's—?"

"Something is wrong with our baby."

"I'll be right there." Steve's voice shifted to the clipped, crisp tone it took on when he was running a meeting. He was in focus mode. "Beth?"

"Yes?"

"I love you."

"I love you too."

An hour later, Steve and I sat perched on upholstered chairs as Dr. Sandler looked at us across his desk. At first, he said nothing, but the tenderness in his eyes and faint knot of his brow said all I needed to know. He was about to crush us. I reached for my husband's hand and felt a squeeze. Steve and I glanced at each other, and the hard set of his jaw told me he, too, was bracing for the worst.

"Beth, Steve, I'm afraid the news is not good." He paused as if to gauge our reactions and whether it was safe to proceed. Four unblinking eyes stared back at him.

"Dr. Daley and I both see conclusive evidence from your ultrasound that your baby has two genetic conditions—Turner's Syndrome and a cystic hygroma."

Two?

Steve's fingers tightened around my hand.

"What does that mean?" Steve asked, his voice flat with fear.

"They are both genetic conditions. With Turner Syndrome, there's a problem with one of the chromosomes." Dr. Sandler paused, and a flicker of some unknown emotion crossed his face. "This issue is compounded by the cystic hygroma—there is a very large sack of fluid on the back of the baby's neck. It's twice the size of the head."

The room went quiet except for the buzz of the fluorescent lights. Steve broke the silence.

"What can be done?"

Dr. Sandler took a deep breath, his slow exhalation like a heavy curtain falling over our dream.

"I'm afraid there's really nothing we can do. Between the two conditions, Dr. Daley and I believe the baby will not likely survive the pregnancy."

"There's *nothing* we can do?" Steve, the brilliant strategist, the master problem-solver, was grasping at any pieces of hope that could be assembled into a solution. But Dr. Sandler's response forced a halt to his reckoning.

"I'm so sorry," Dr. Sandler said, his voice cracking.

Rain is typical in Florida in June. As I glanced away from Dr. Sandler and looked out the window, huge raindrops began to fall. White puffy clouds shifted to the east, and a gray mass took its place, rolling across the sky as if God was pulling the covers over our town. Within minutes, the slow cadence of droplets became a fierce drumroll as Dr. Sandler sat with us and explained our options.

A few more questions, a few more foreboding answers. There was nothing left for Steve and me to do, it seemed, but to terminate the pregnancy. Our baby was going to die.

The downpour outside made me feel like God was crying with us. I sat there feeling my wholeness slip away. Suddenly, my skin was just a container for broken pieces—me, my baby. And then the question appeared and invaded me like a virus:

Will I ever have a healthy baby?

I broke the news to my mother, and she hopped on a plane. Two days after the ultrasound, the three of us drove to the hospital in near-total silence. As Steve pulled into the parking space, I found myself just sitting there, not wanting to get out of the car. This couldn't be it. More than anything in the world, I wanted a child to nurture. The intense yearning to marry and grow a family had taken me over. To find the perfect someone to walk through life with and together create a safe and loving home for children. Motherhood tugged on me like a magnet. Everything was coming together like some kind of divine plan that culminated in this baby, and now it was all being taken away.

My door opened. Steve leaned in and offered me his hand. I sighed, then unbuckled my seatbelt and climbed out.

Check-in was at 9:00 a.m. From the front desk, a nurse escorted us to a private room in the labor and delivery wing. *Babies are supposed to be born here*, I thought as we trudged down the corridor, *not die.*

I watched the nurse insert the syringe into my IV then slowly depress the plunger. The Pitocin would induce labor. I just had to sit and wait for the contractions to start. It could take a few hours, or it could take all day.

I sat on the bed like so many other expectant mothers before, in a hospital gown dotted with tiny blue flowers. The raised metal rails on either side of me felt like prison bars. Minutes, then hours ticked past, mostly in silence. Steve would stand up and stretch, pace for a minute, then sit back down in the armchair by the bed. Periodically, Mom wandered over to hold my hand. There was a stack of magazines on the table next to me. *Newsweek, National Geographic.* I would pick one up, flip through it for a minute, then put it down and take another. I tried to doze off, but my mind spun wildly like a top on the verge of tipping, so I mostly just stared out of the window at the palm trees swaying in the breeze.

Why is this happening? What could possibly be God's purpose in all of this?

The silence around me was broken by a hesitant rap on the door. As it opened, I saw the welcome face of our pastor, The Reverend Woody, peek in. Reverend Woody had performed our wedding ceremony at Siesta Key Chapel, and now, he seemed out of context in this stale, sterile hospital room. Since I'd known him, Dr. Woody had been a pillar of strength through my move to Florida, marriage to Steve, and pregnancy just months later. Now, he would support us again in this time of trial.

Dr. Woody entered the room, and Steve rose to shake his hand. After a nod to my mother, Reverend Woody stood to my right while Steve took a place to my left. The three of us bowed our heads and joined hands as Dr. Woody began to pray, "Lord, we are saddened and confused. Please be with Beth and Steve as they mourn the loss of this precious child of God . . ." After a moment of silence, Reverend Woody slipped out of the room, leaving a trail of his love in our midst.

And we continued to wait.

After eight interminable hours, I began to wonder if it was ever going to happen. *I can't take this anymore. How much longer?*

Then instantly, a thought came to me.

The angel.

I sat upright with such a jolt that Steve and my mother startled. "Steve, would you mind grabbing my bag over there?"

He rose and retrieved it from the cabinet where I had piled my things and handed it to me. I reached inside and pulled out a small ceramic figurine—an angel that my childhood friend, Gina, had given me. "Always look to angels, Beth," she had told me. "They're all around, and they are here to help you." I closed my eyes and pressed the angel to my heart then placed it on the table next to me.

Within moments, my abdomen constricted. Contractions had begun. Ten minutes later, under the watchful gaze of that ornamental angel, our first child was born. As Dr. Sandler predicted, the baby did not survive the birth. They wrapped the tiny child, a little girl, in a hospital blanket and handed the delicate bundle of sadness to Steve. I lay back exhausted on the pillows and watched him hold the lifeless form of our child, no bigger than his hand.

Yet even in that boundless sorrow, I somehow felt God's presence. It was a blessing our baby did not have to come into this world and for hours or even seconds, know only struggle. I lacked an understanding of why this was happening but did not doubt that, as my husband cradled our child's body, her soul was in divine hands.

———

The season of late spring, with its delicate warmth and welcome breezes, was slipping into a sweltering summer. Normally, the ferocious humidity was something I sought to avoid, but in the days and weeks following the loss of our child, I welcomed the heat. Once I was able, I hit the road running. Feet pounding, tears pouring from my eyes, I made my sorrow an offering to the blazing fire of the Florida heat.

Our baby never had a name or a burial. No one suggested it, and since I had not walked that agonizing path before, it never occurred to me that these rituals and ways of honoring her may have helped. Instead, every day under the burning sun, I purged sweat and tears mixed in a salty stream over my face and neck. *This is how life is now*, I thought. *I'll mourn every moment into forever.*

Dr. Sandler had tried to reassure me that I could still bear a healthy child, telling me the conflation of two genetic issues was a fluke and unlikely to happen again. Still, I wondered if the experience of mother-hood I so longed for was a prize that would elude me. I wanted to experience life with children, to go to all the magical places I knew they could take me. Had that wondrous kingdom closed its gates to me?

Somehow, as the months passed and the summer rains shifted to a drier hot fall, my grief began to fade. Time's passage began to heal my heart. It was unnoticeable at first, yet every day, a fraction of strength returned to me, and by the time we entered autumn, the nights became easier. Sleep returned, and as the sun rose every morning, I felt new hope begin to blossom as we tried again to conceive.

Still, nearly a year later, we had no luck. The burdensome thoughts that held me down after my miscarriage began to weigh on me once more. My older sister, Tracy, had even shared with me a way to determine when you are ovulating. She instructed me to take my temperature before getting out of bed every morning and fill in the chart that would predict the brief window when conception was possible.

Every month that I learned I was not pregnant, the wound left by our baby's passing was torn open again. What would my life become if I couldn't have a child? I had already abandoned my banking career to be a mother. If I couldn't serve in that way, there must be some other path to create the meaning and purpose I so longed for. I began thinking about going back to college for social work and started studying for the entrance exams.

Then, just like that, as miracles do, it happened. As Steve and I stared at the dull purple plus sign on the little plastic stick, waves of shock and gratitude stunned us into silence.

That night as I lay tucked in bed with Steve by my side, I felt the unmistakable calm that arrives in the presence of grace. Once again, there was a life inside me, cells dividing and growing, forming into a vessel for a holy little being. God had not forgotten me.

With everything that had happened, though, fear was a constant companion, lurking like a shadow. As we approached the sixteen-week ultrasound and blood tests, my anxiety mounted.

"Beth, everything's looking great," Dr. Sandler said. "I really don't think we need to do an amniocentesis."

"I know, Dr. Sandler," I said. In the manufactured light of the exam room, his tennis tan washed into a pale beige. "I understand it might add some risk to the pregnancy, but I have to know for sure."

"Okay, then," he said as he nodded slowly. "Let's go ahead and get it scheduled within the next week."

Days later, with the overhead lights down low, Dr. Sandler studied the images from the ultrasound as the nurse handed him a syringe. "Okay, Beth. First, you'll feel a little sting. Then a second poke as it goes into your uterus." I nodded and took a deep breath as a long needle plunged slowly into my abdomen. *Please*, my heart again pleaded as I watched the syringe fill with pale yellow fluid.

Over the next few days, I wore ruts in the sidewalks around my neighborhood. I struggled to sit still and anything requiring focus, especially on my pregnancy, was a challenge. Over and over, I picked up my copy of *What to Expect When You're Expecting* only to put it down again.

One evening as I stood by the stove stirring pasta into a pot, the phone rang. My body jumped, sending a thin spray of water off the end of the wooden spoon. I hustled to the phone.

"Hello?"

"Mrs. Knopik?" a woman's voice asked.

"Yes, this is she."

"Hi, Mrs. Knopik, this is Dr. Sandler's office."

"Yes, hi!" In my other hand, I felt my grip on the spoon tighten.

"I have good news. The results of your amniocentesis are in, and everything looks just fine. We wanted to let you know right away."

"Oh my, God," I said, collapsing against the wall. "Thank you. This is the best news ever."

I hung up and fireworks exploded in my chest. I realized in that moment just how much I had been holding back from connecting to my pregnancy and the baby inside me. As my walls of insecurity came crashing down, I felt myself united with the joy I so longed to feel.

I turned from the phone and looked out the big picture window in our family room and saw that clouds had begun to clear from a summer storm. Something to the right of the scene tugged at my attention. A rainbow. A bold, brilliant coalescing of color that felt as if it was a message sent directly to me. *God is here.*

Then I remembered Steve and rushed back to the phone.

"Oh, thank the Lord!" he exclaimed, followed by a massive exhalation. We had not talked about it much—maybe because we didn't want to dwell on the negative—but after what had happened last time, doubt had become a constant companion for us both.

Then I told Steve about the rainbow. "I want to have one painted on the wall of the nursery," I said. The nursery we had not yet begun to decorate, just in case.

"That's a great idea. Oh man, I'm just so relieved. Maybe now I can get some work done," he laughed.

Even with this news, though, I still worried about the baby. In the time that had passed since my first pregnancy, we had moved from the condo to a house. One day, I was adding chlorine tablets to our pool and, though I thought I was being careful, a plume of fumes burst from the bucket of tablets, blasting my face and filling my lungs as I gasped.

Oh no! Oh, God, please don't let those chemicals harm the baby.

For hours, I obsessed over whether chlorine fumes could damage a fetus. Finally, I pried myself from the couch and walked outside to retrieve the mail. I opened the front door and had just crossed the threshold when I came to a sudden stop. My mouth fell open. An explosion of color stretched across the sky before me. Tears escaped my eyes as I beheld the rainbow.

Thank you, God. Thank you.

God was telling me my baby was okay. And then I knew, beyond any doubt, that rainbows were more than just beautiful natural phenomena. For me, at least, they were an assurance of divine presence.

Still, from that day on, I was extra careful. I rested as much as I could, took care when I exercised to not let my heart rate get too high, and ate healthy foods. Close to the end of my pregnancy, I lay on my bed at night, and Steve and I would watch as the baby's kicks caused a roll of motion across my abdomen.

Though I had always been drawn outside to walk, to run, and to meditate, in the last two weeks of my pregnancy, I found myself nesting inside, creating a snug, secluded refuge for my baby. I decorated the crib with colorful lions, hippos, and giraffes in shades of blue, pink, and teal. I washed cotton onesies in a special mild soap and stacked newborn diapers on the changing table. I dusted the baseboards, mopped the floors, and washed hooded bath towels. I was ready.

March 14, 1996 was a sunny morning in Sarasota. With beads of sweat on my forehead and Steve as my coach, after a final hour of labor, our second daughter, Leanna Mae Knopik, came easily into the world. A nurse held her up for Steve and me to glimpse, then our tiny, crying girl was quickly bundled in a cotton hospital blanket, and a pink knit cap was placed on her head.

Afterward, I lay there in my yellow velour pajamas with the gold angel pin secured to the collar, marveling at Leanna's beauty. Swaddled in a blanket and resting against Steve's chest, she was barely larger than a football. When she nestled in my arms, a pervasive calm swept over me. It was the greatest joy and the deepest peace I had ever known.

During those two days in the hospital, Leanna's bassinet was always empty. I longed to hold her, stroke her fine, fuzzy blonde hair, and watch as she tried to open her tiny eyes.

When all of the tests were done and the nurses finally confirmed that everything was as it should be, I let the last wash of gratitude overcome me. We did it. My beautiful baby was here, and our journey together could really begin.

Our first evening home from the hospital, I gazed out the kitchen window to see Steve on the patio by the pool cradling Leanna against his chest. They were framed by our brilliant purple azaleas, whose blossoms peaked early that year, just in time to welcome Leanna home. Beyond our yard was a nature preserve, and as I looked on, the last golden light of dusk was glistening on the reeds as they swayed in the breeze. *Moments don't get more perfect than this*, I thought.

That night, Steve cooked a special meal he had been planning for weeks—steaks on the grill with a special mushroom sauce. As we sat down to eat, lights dimmed, Steve's voice was almost a whisper when he said, "I wish my mom was still alive to see her."

"She's here," I said. "I know it. She's surrounding us with her love. Maybe Leanna has her soul."

Steve looked down at his plate for a long moment then smiled at his daughter, swaddled in a blanket on the sofa, sleeping peacefully. "I sure wish she would hurry and grow up so I could have a conversation with her. I can't wait!"

"Steve," I warned, "don't wish her life away. She'll grow up fast enough." I wanted to stop time, to freeze the moment so I could savor it forever.

Steve turned and reached behind him, then handed me a shiny black box tied with a white ribbon. I stared at him, feeling my lips curl into a smile.

"It's for you," he said, nudging the box toward me. "Well, sort of. Open it."

Slowly, I untied the ribbon and opened the box. Three diamonds on a gold chain sparkled up at me.

"June made it," Steve said, referring to a friend of ours. "You can wear this until the day Leanna has a baby of her own. Then it becomes hers."

I put the necklace around my neck, soaking in the loving gesture, yet I found myself unable to picture such a distant future.

As parents, we take so much for granted. Our children will get married. Our children will have children of their own. All these hopes and dreams we build on the assumption that our children will grow to become adults.

Chapter 2

Nearly midnight, Steve and I pulled into the parking garage at All Children's Hospital. We walked swiftly to the front entrance of the hospital and approached the welcome desk. "We're the parents of Leanna Knopik. She was just brought in by helicopter."

The receptionist's mouth shifted from a kind smile to a stern look as she turned to her monitor. "Of course. Spell your last name please?" A few quick taps on the keyboard. "Yes, she's here. ICU is on the fifth floor. The elevators are down the hall and to the left. Here are your visitors' badges. You'll need to check in every time you visit."

Steve and I wound our way through corridors covered with bright murals. When we stepped off the elevator and turned the first corner, we spotted Leanna right away. She was not in a room yet but off to the side of a central area, propped up in a large rolling bed with heavy side rails. A doctor was at her side checking her pulse. He looked up, "Great, this looks like Mom and Dad now."

"Leanna," I leaned over her, "how are you feeling?" Steve stood across from me on the other side of her bed.

"Okay, I guess," One side of Leanna's mouth curved slightly. Her eyelids drooped as she rested her head against the pillow.

"Don't worry, sweet pea," I said, brushing a sandy strand of hair from her eye. "We're going to get you all taken care of. How was the helicopter ride?"

"It was so weird," she replied, rolling her eyes with a wrinkled brow. "But the people were really nice."

We turned our attention to the doctor—a lean, smiling man in blue scrubs. He extended his hand. "Dr. Everett," he said as we shook hands. "I'm the cardiologist." He reached across and took Steve's hand briefly then looked down at Leanna. Dr. Everett's voice was softly accented and, as if expecting me to ask, he added, "I'm originally from South Africa."

Suddenly in the distance, a frantic beeping erupted. A nurse appeared then rushed into a room behind us. Through the picture window, I saw her push a series of buttons on a machine with long cords like spider legs that disappeared under the blankets where a baby rested. The beeps stopped. I looked back to Dr. Everett.

"I've got the notes from Sarasota Memorial," he continued, "and we've started running some tests. It's probably going to be a bit of a long night while we get results and figure out our game plan, but rest assured, your daughter is in good hands. It's likely that this is a virus, and Leanna just needs some help fighting it." He looked back and forth between Steve and me as he spoke, then he turned to Leanna. "We're going to make sure you don't spend any more of your summer than you have to in this place, okay? You'll be back to . . ."

"Rowing," Leanna said, "and a church conference and a Coldplay concert—"

Dr. Everett smiled. "Just as I figured. Well, we'll do our best to get you back to all of that as soon as we can, okay?"

"Yes," I nodded. "Absolutely."

I looked at Steve, whose eyelids drooped from exhaustion. He was nodding as well.

In short order, the nurses transferred Leanna into a room in the ICU. That night, Steve and I settled as best we could into two blue vinyl chairs that reclined into makeshift beds. We slept in bursts. Every time I drifted off, it seemed I was asleep for no more than twenty or thirty minutes before a piercing noise startled me back to consciousness. A nurse would swoop in, offer a smile, and press a series of buttons on one of the machines monitoring Leanna's vital signs. One nurse with rich cocoa skin looked so young she could have been one of Leanna's classmates in high school, but she moved with such confidence, checking readouts and making notes, I couldn't help but feel reassured. We were in the right place. Leanna would get the care she needed, and everything would be okay.

I pulled the hospital blanket up over my shoulders and propped my head against the pillow so I could watch Leanna as she slept. Somehow, she seemed peaceful despite the wires and cords she was now connected to. The last time Leanna had been in a hospital overnight was when she was born. I remembered watching the nurse prick her heel and hearing Leanna cry out, her tiny foot turning red as the nurse squeezed out a few droplets of blood for the genetic screening. "Stop!" I wanted to yell. I felt each of Leanna's cries as if the pain was my own. I just wanted to hold my baby forever, to keep her safe from everything. It all felt so fragile in those early days. This tiny person so dependent on us.

Looking at Leanna now, she seemed vulnerable again, not like the robust teen I knew. Only this time, I knew that nothing in my power could help her; gone were the days when the simple act of holding her seemed to ward away all that could harm her. *Please, God*, I thought as my own eyes started to close, *heal my daughter.*

The next morning, I woke early to the sound of Leanna's voice. "Pretty good," she was saying to a nurse I had not seen before. The dark veil of night was lifting as the sun began to brighten the room. I had just thought to scan for Steve when he appeared in the doorway holding a cardboard tray with two coffee cups in one hand and a paper bag in the other.

"Hospital's finest," he said with a smirk as he set everything down on a small side table. Despite his dull tone, I knew he was joking. There was something about the weak coffee and parched pastries that delivered a twinge in my heart for my husband. Steve, who was always in control, a man whose tall stature, impeccable demeanor, and shrewd decisiveness had earned him a respectable reputation among all who knew him. A leader in the community and in our state, Steve had risen to the role of CEO for one of the state's largest retailers, in large part because of his steady, easy confidence and elegance. This was a person whose life revolved around making major decisions with an air of certainty. Here, in the hostile blue vinyl chair, sipping subpar coffee, he seemed just as helpless as anyone. His bloodshot eyes and scruffy beard added to his helplessness and compounded my own fears. There was nothing he couldn't solve. Until there was this.

"I saw Dr. Everett in the hall," Steve said. "He's going to come and talk to us."

I sat up. "Did he tell you anything?"

Steve shook his head as he took a sip. I reached for the other coffee. "I gave Greg Simmons a call to let him know what was going on," he said. Greg was a cardiac surgeon and one of Steve's childhood friends. "Also, Chris and Maureen are here."

"Wow, really?" Chris, Steve's younger brother, and his girlfriend, Maureen, were partners in a law firm. "Aren't they busy? Where are they?"

"They're out in the main waiting room. Chris plans to hang out for the day. Maureen is going back to their place to make us some food."

"Steve, they don't have to—"

"I told them that, but they really want to help. If you're up to it, you can go out and say hi after Dr. Everett comes in. But they said not to worry about them; they just want to be here if we need anything."

"Good morning." As if on cue, Dr. Everett appeared at the door. His fresh face suggested he had a full night's sleep, though I knew that was impossible. We had seen him just—I looked at my watch—six hours before. "How are you feeling, Leanna?" he asked as he reached for a clipboard at the foot of her bed.

"Tired," Leanna responded, offering a faint smile. "But okay, I guess."

"Well, that's no surprise. Your body is really fighting something." Dr. Everett looked down at the clipboard, flipped through a few pages, then dropped it back into a metal slot at the foot of the bed. He slid the stethoscope from around his neck. "Okay if I take a listen?" he asked. Leanna nodded. Steve and I gathered by Leanna's bedside as the doctor checked her heart and lungs. "Okay," he finally said, again draping the stethoscope around his neck and turning to us. "So here's where we are. The tests aren't conclusive, but we feel certain Leanna has a virus. We don't yet know which one for sure, but that won't stop us from treating her. We can support her body to fight it more effectively." He took turns looking at Steve and me as he spoke, then he turned to Leanna. "You'll probably have to be with us for a few days so we can get you taken care of. Okay?"

Leanna nodded. "Yeah. Sure."

"Alright then," Dr. Everett said. He turned back to Steve and me. "Mom, Dad, I'll keep checking in with you as we know more. I hope to have some information from the lab shortly. In the meantime, let the nurses know if there's anything you need."

Normally, I try to stay present and not anticipate what may happen. Yoga practice and my holistic doctor, Caryn Young, had taught me that. But as I stood there and looked at my daughter, something didn't feel right. Something was whispering in my ear words I couldn't make out but that filled my stomach with dread.

Be calm, I told myself, taking a deep breath. *She had the flu last year and got over it. She's strong. Everything will be fine.*

I turned to my husband after Dr. Everett exited the room. "Do you think we should call Rogers?"

He thought for a minute. "Why don't we wait a day or two until we know more. I'm sure he's having the time of his life, and I don't want to worry him unnecessarily. Plus, the counselors don't want the kids to be on their phones."

———

Three years after Leanna was born, Rogers came along. When we went from three to four, our family felt complete. I remembered Leanna presenting her new baby brother with a plush toy she'd picked out. Beaming, she thrust the alligator at him. Steve and I laughed as the four of us huddled together in the hospital bed while my mom snapped a picture.

Leanna adored her brother and filled the big sister role proudly. She often covered him with a baby blanket during his naps and fed him his first solid food using a coated spoon. But early on, it was evident that our children were very different from one another. Leanna was thoughtful and quiet and Rogers, sensitive and bold. At age six, Rogers played Spiderman in a summer camp talent show. With twenty parents watching, he clambered up a chain-link fence, but he climbed too high and ended up toppling over the other side. I rushed over in a panic, but thankfully, only his pride was bruised.

Now in his teens, Rogers was still a showman. This summer at his performing arts camp, he had landed the role of the minstrel in "Once Upon a Mattress." Rehearsals were well underway and in a couple of weeks, he would be stepping out on stage and into the spotlight, something he loved to do. Provided Leanna was well enough by then, we would all be flying up to see him perform.

"Yeah, you're right," I nodded to Steve. "We'll call him when we know more."

Meanwhile, confined to her hospital bed, Leanna was getting anxious. She was fully conscious and alert and tired of being cooped up. "I can't *wait* to get out of here," she complained.

Word had gotten around quickly that Leanna was back from camp and in the hospital. Her friends wanted to know what was going on. My phone buzzed constantly, signaling Facebook messages and direct texts. When my phone lit up and I saw *Rogers*, my breath caught.

Mom, what's going on with Leanna? Someone said they saw on Facebook that she's in the hospital??

I clapped a hand to my forehead. *Ugh, Facebook!* In trying to reassure everyone that Leanna was okay, I had put a short post on Facebook, not even thinking that Rogers would get wind of it.

Your sister is okay, I texted back. *She's got the flu. But she should be out of here in a few days.*

Are you sure?

Yes, don't worry.

Alrighty, well . . . Tell her I'm thinking of her, okay?

I will, Rog. But really, don't worry. Everything is fine. God is watching over all of us.

The messages from Leanna's friends kept coming. "Leanna," I sighed at one point, "Can I take a picture and send it to your friends so that they can see you're okay."

"Seriously?" Leanna protested. "I don't have any mascara on, and my hair is probably—"

"Leanna, you're *beautiful*. Please?"

"Fine, Mom," she said, playfully rolling her eyes. I leaned over Leanna's bed as she offered a tired grin.

Click.

It was the last photo I ever took of Leanna.

———

"We're calling it *myocarditis*. The virus has gotten into Leanna's heart, and that's why her vitals have been so difficult to stabilize. When a virus invades the heart in this way, it gets inflamed and makes it a bit more challenging for the heart to pump blood through the body." Even though the news felt grim, Dr. Everett maintained his positive demeanor.

"What does this mean?" I asked. The three of us stood in the hall outside of Leanna's room. Steve and I were about to head outside for some fresh air while Leanna slept.

"We will try to treat Leanna with medications," Dr. Everett said, "but there's one other thing I need to talk to you about—we'd like to do a biopsy to try and determine which virus this is."

"A biopsy?" My hand fluttered to my chest, covering my own heart. My daughter had been doodling little hearts next to her name since she'd learned to write it. For years, she had filled margins of notepads and school papers with hearts. In Leanna's room at home, her white chenille bedspread was covered in colorful hearts, as were the hand-painted borders of her room. Even the drawer pulls on her dresser were hearts, and more hearts adorned the walls of her bathroom. And here, now, the doctor was telling me they needed to take a specimen of her heart.

Yes, okay, cut into my daughter's heart. It felt as unnatural a consent as a parent could give. Yet Steve and I gave our go-ahead. What else could we do?

That afternoon the nurses bustled around, preparing Leanna for the procedure. "Mrs. Knopik?" one of them said.

"Yes?"

"I'm going to need to remove Leanna's bracelets for the biopsy."

I nodded. "Okay."

A few minutes later, as a small team of medical staff wheeled Leanna out of the room, one turned and walked back to me, arm outstretched. "Here you go, Mom," she said, handing me a clear plastic bag. Inside it were Leanna's bracelets, a worn woven friendship bracelet she had made a few months before and had never taken off, and a small silver bracelet I had given her on Valentine's Day with the word *LOVE* engraved on it.

Steve and I followed along next to Leanna and her medical entourage as far as they allowed. We watched as a tall, strapping physician assistant smiled back at us then reached forward and pressed a square metal plate on the wall. A set of doors whooshed open and, just like that, our daughter disappeared down the hall.

We trudged back to an empty room and sat. Side by side, we waited. There was nothing to say, nothing to do. Finally, I bowed my head. *Please, God, heal my daughter.* I made that my silent refrain.

"Beth, Steve?" I looked up to find a tall, willowy man whose thin beard did nothing to disguise his boyish smile.

"Hi, Clay," Steve said, standing and offering his hand.

Clay Thomas was our associate pastor at First Presbyterian Church, but thanks to his upbeat nature and playful disposition, people often assumed he was the youth minister. I had texted Clay earlier in the day to let him know what was going on. When Steve and I did not respond to his calls or texts, he had hopped in the car and drove forty-five minutes to the hospital. How he found us through the maze of halls and elevators to the small, distant waiting room was a mystery, but it was also like Clay. We had not known him all that well up to that point, yet one thing I noted about him, in addition to his fun-loving personality, he just seemed to find a way to make things happen.

Clay took Steve's hand and rested the other on Steve's shoulder. I stood and Clay turned and gave me a brief hug.

Clay had come equipped with a stack of magazines to help us pass the time. I guess pastors were used to the hospital waiting game, though the last thing I could imagine doing at that moment was read. Clay also prayed with us, offering an eloquent plea on Leanna's and our behalf. Then he pointed out that others would probably welcome the chance to pray for us, as well.

"You know, folks at church will want to know how Leanna's doing, but clearly, you don't need the burden of calling or texting everyone.

There's a website called CaringBridge for people with ill family members. You can post updates, and everyone can just go there to see what's happening with Leanna."

"Okay," I nodded. "Thanks, Clay." I was already overwhelmed with all the texts and emails from family and friends.

Not long after, Dr. Everett appeared and assured us that everything had gone well with the biopsy and Leanna would be back in her room shortly.

The following day, I made my first post on CaringBridge.

Welcome to our CaringBridge site. We've created it to keep friends and family updated. We appreciate your support and words of hope and encouragement during this time when it matters most . . .

From then on, my goal was to post every day.

All the while, Chris and Maureen were a constant presence and blessed us with homemade meals and healthy salads. Chris took on the duty of texting detailed updates to family. As medical malpractice attorneys, they could understand and explain the hospital jargon better than Steve or I could, and I was relieved to not have to worry about it.

After another day or so of waiting, the pathology report came back. The biopsy confirmed the overall diagnosis of myocarditis but provided precious little additional information. After testing Leanna's heart tissue for ten different viruses, the pathologists were unable to determine which one had invaded her heart. The following day, the hospital moved Leanna to the cardiovascular intensive care unit so she could receive more specialized care.

Flowers were forbidden at All Children's. The nurses said the smell could cause issues for patients with allergies. When I noted the prohibition of flowers on CaringBridge, Leanna's room filled with gifts. Multi-colored balloons tied to a small weight hovered in one corner. Every day, another stack of cards arrived. There were jigsaw puzzles, crystals said to have healing powers, and holy water in a clear glass bottle. A giant poster proclaiming, "WE CARE!" and signed by folks from our church hung on the door. Steve and I put up framed photos of Leanna, including one of her taken that Easter where we had gone out for brunch; she sat perched between Rogers and Josh. Lastly, on the wall, Steve and I taped the bright pink t-shirt that Leanna had made for her mission trip. From where she lay in her bed, Leanna could read the verse she had so painstakingly traced:

> *Do not be conformed to this world but continually be transformed by the renewal of your minds so that you will be able to determine what God's will is—what is proper, praising and perfect.*
>
> *Romans 12:2*

We hoped it would provide some sense of support. For her part, Leanna tried to stay positive, but we could tell the ordeal was starting to wear on her, even beyond the lethargy caused by the virus.

"Dad, I'm hungry. Can I pleeeaasse have a smoothie?" she pleaded. She was receiving nutrition intravenously, and the doctors had forbidden us to give her anything else.

"Can't she have a smoothie?" Steve asked Dr. Everett. "Even just a few sips?"

"I know it's hard," Dr. Everett replied, "but Leanna is in a delicate position. We're not sure what tests or procedures she might need in the next forty-eight hours, so it's best to keep her stomach empty."

Our daughter's only request, and we could not fulfill it.

———

It had been four days since Leanna was admitted to All Children's. For four endless nights, Steve and I dozed fitfully on vinyl chairs. The second day, Steve went home to retrieve toiletries and fresh clothes, and at some point, we each grabbed a shower in the bathroom down the hall from Leanna's room.

As I continued to post on CaringBridge, I was cautious about what I shared and how I shared it. A lot of people were reading the updates, including Leanna's friends, and I did not want them to become unnecessarily worried. It was evident now that my daughter was critically ill, but positivity was an essential part of my nature, so I tried to keep the posts upbeat. I had my concerns, but we needed to keep our hope strong.

It was during the fourth night that my resolve first began to waver. I was pacing back and forth at the foot of Leanna's bed, unable to sit still because her heart rate was so unstable. The monitors menaced: 150 one minute, then 165, 148, 162, jumping erratically like my own heart that quivered with worry. The nurses hustled around the bed, murmuring to one another. They stopped making eye contact with me.

Propped up in bed, eyes wide and breathing labored, Leanna stared ahead at the black TV screen on the wall. I saw her body arch slightly as she struggled to take a breath, panic in her eyes. I rushed to an open spot next to her. "It's okay, sweetheart. I'm here."

I shot a plaintive look at one of the nurses across the bed. She was holding a syringe, about to inject something into Leanna's IV. "This will help her rest," she said, her voice just above a whisper.

As I watched Leanna drift off to sleep, my anxiety escalated. What was happening to my little girl? Prisoners of hope, Steve and I became obsessed with the fluctuations in Leanna's heart. We sat there hour after hour staring at the blazing red digits as they climbed then dropped. Fear consumed me.

At one point, I texted Clay.

I'm so afraid.

His reply was quick, just a few moments later. *Do you want me to come up?*

No, it's okay. She's a little better right now. Part of me wanted the distraction and the reassurance of his presence, but what I needed most of all was sleep.

Okay, he texted back. *I pray that Leanna will be surrounded by angels tonight.*

Chapter 3

The clock on the wall read 10:37 p.m. Deep sleep was impossible in the wretched chairs; they were far too small and stiff. Instead, I twisted and turned and shifted into one cramped position after another. *Why is it always so cold in here?* I wondered. *Wouldn't you want people to be more comfortable? And the cotton blankets are so thin.*

Four days and nights of doctors, nurses, and institutional chairs were taking their toll. At night, the nurses were quiet, gliding in on their soft-soled shoes, but the screeching of the electronic devices never stopped. I knew I should feel grateful for the machines surrounding my daughter's bed. They were giving the medical team critical information. They were keeping Leanna hydrated and supplying vital nutrition. The alarms were designed to save her life should something suddenly change for the worse. Still, even when they were not beeping, the flashing numbers and fluctuating waves held me in the grip of constant tension as I braced for whatever the next moment might bring. The alarms sounded several times an hour, and when they were not sounding, I was waiting for them to go off. Every time Steve or I began to drift off, an ear-splitting tone startled us back to wakefulness.

As I struggled to cope with exhaustion, my prayers, too, became ragged. A desperate bargaining instead of relying on God's plan. I wanted to be able to heal Leanna myself, but I was forced to put her in the care of this unseen force so much greater and more capable than I. And so, I begged, each prayer delivering me from one minute to the next. I longed for the days of saying prayers together with Leanna at night, sitting at her bedside, talking to God together.

Everyone who knew Leanna would tell you that she was a sweet and caring person, even a bit quirky. For someone her age, she was unusually dedicated to showing her commitment to God and to others through good works, not just good words. That's why she had traveled to West Virginia, embarking on a mission trip to help those in need. That's why she did so much of what she did, from walking in an all-night Relay for Life cancer fundraiser to using a precious day off from school to deliver food and clothing to poor farmworkers. While her peers were at the beach or the mall, Leanna served people who needed it.

My daughter was always a bit of an enigma. She had such a goofy and playful way about her, yet from her earliest days, she also embodied a seriousness that has made me feel perhaps there was something more to her presence on this earth. In some ways, growing up, she never really seemed like a child but more of a wise soul who knew more than her years let on. Once, as a three-year-old, she was drawing on a little whiteboard with some markers. I watched as a face appeared, smiling with curly hair.

"That's a beautiful picture, Leanna," I said.

She turned to me, a serious look on her face. "That was my husband," she said. "He was very good to me."

———

I studied Leanna lying there in the hospital bed. *Always my baby but so big now. Where did the years go?* As I considered this mature, developed human before me, I struggled to remember our last conversation. Words I'd taken for granted then would have flooded me with euphoria now.

When was the last time we really talked?

I looked down at my phone and begin to scroll through my text thread with my daughter. I smiled as I discovered one from me to her in May timestamped 11:22 p.m.

Are you still awake?

Just finishing my paper, she'd written back.

Go to bed! I replied. *You need your sleep.*

In Leanna's teen years, our chats became few and far between. She was a dedicated student, and when Leanna started high school in the International Baccalaureate program, she began to stay up late to keep up with the heavy load of nightly homework, her books spread out all over her bed.

I thought of all those nighttime prayers we said together when she was a child, how we ended the day with gratitude for blessings received or requests for support hundreds, probably thousands of times.

Now I lay me down to sleep,
I pray the Lord my soul to keep.
If I should die before I wake,
I pray the Lord my soul to take.

The vinyl of the hospital chair creaked as I sat up, abandoning my attempt at sleep. I looked across the room at Leanna and again longed to sit on the edge of her bed. To cradle her in my arms the way I did when she had a sore throat or a fever. But the rails and machines made it impossible. My baby girl was out of reach.

At some point, I dozed off, but my sleep ended abruptly as overhead lights flicked on above me. An assortment of doctors and nurses moved in a tight hustle around Leanna's bed. Something was terribly wrong.

I glanced first at the clock, which signaled 3:00 a.m., then at Steve, who was sitting upright. More staff barreled into the room armed with trays of medical instruments, syringes, and supplies.

"Beth? Steve?" Denise, one of Leanna's nurses, stood over us. "I'm afraid I have to ask you to step out into the hall for a bit. We just need to do a few things to help Leanna. Dr. Andrews, the intensivist, is on his way."

"What's going on?" Steve asked, his brows trenched in what had become a perpetual frown.

"Dr. Andrews will explain everything," she said, gently motioning to the doorway.

I turned back to Leanna's bed. She was invisible behind the swarm of scrubs. I was at once amazed by the staff's efficiency and slightly offended by our banishment.

I felt Steve's hand on my back as he led me into the hall. We settled into a pair of rolling office chairs that had been stationed just outside the door. We both leaned forward, elbows resting on our knees, waiting for Dr. Andrews to tell us what was happening with our daughter. Behind the closed door to the room that held our daughter, a team of medical experts moved swiftly, efficiently, with purpose. As I scanned the hallway, I was struck by the juxtaposition: the nurse's station lolled with quiet as these nurses awaited a call. The frantic commotion of our room contrasted with the still calm of the corridor. I glanced down at the newly polished floor tiles, and my mind wandered.

———

Leanna is six years old and Rogers, three. Steve and I take them on a four-day Disney cruise to the Bahamas. One night, Steve and Rogers go to bed early, leaving Leanna and me on the balcony outside our stateroom. There we are, perched four stories above the ocean, surrounded by a vast darkness of sea and sky. Lights glimmer in the wake of the massive ship as it slides silently forward.

I am resting with my elbows propped on the railing when I look over and see Leanna in her pink pajamas, perched on a chair, hoping to get a better view. She leans forward toward the railing, and my heart races as I picture her slipping over it and into the abyss below. In an instant, I pluck her off the chair and bundle her inside. I sit there on the bed cradling her against my pounding chest while over long minutes, my breathing finally returns to normal.

———

"I'm not sure what's happening, but it seems serious." Steve's voice into the phone made the cruise ship's stateroom disappear, and I was back at the hospital. He turned to me and whispered, "Clay" then continued talking.

"They're doing something, I'm not sure what. We're waiting for the doctor to come and talk to us."

As if summoned, Dr. Andrews slipped out of Leanna's room then took a knee in front of us.

"I'll call you back." Steve pocketed his phone.

Dr. Andrews took in a deep breath before speaking. "Leanna is having trouble breathing. We need to intubate her." Out of the corner of my eye, I saw Steve stiffen. "We're going to insert a tube in her windpipe that will help her breathe normally and take a load off of her heart. However . . ." The doctor paused. "Because of Leanna's weakened state, there is a chance this procedure will put her into cardiac arrest. You need to go in and tell her you love her."

Dr. Andrews's voice was soft, and I knew he was trying to be gentle, but his words hit me like a wrecking ball.

Oh, God. Please, God, please. Please don't take my precious girl.

Tears rolled down my cheeks as Steve stood and reached for me. I looked up and his face was frozen. I shook my head. "I can't."

Steve looked at me for a moment, then he disappeared into the room. I began to pace around and around in a tight, frantic circle. *No. No, this is not happening. Cardiac arrest?*

Finally, Steve emerged. He came to me, and we clung to each other, my face buried in his chest. His words rained down on me like a storm cloud. "The team is waiting to perform the procedure. You need to go in there."

The pressure building in me finally exploded. "I *can't*! I don't want her to see me like this!"

Steve was unflinching, his voice firm. "You *have* to go in there."

I filled my lungs and drew the sleeve of my sweatshirt across my face. *Of course, he's right. This could be the last time I see my daughter.* I turned toward the door then paused and bowed my head.

God, please help me to go in and be strong. Please give me the words I need to comfort Leanna.

There was a box at the door filled with surgical masks with images of teddy bears. I picked one up and slipped the loops over my ears. It had become part of procedure—putting on a mask to be close to my daughter. The room was tense, the lights bright. Four medical workers flanked Leanna's bed, two on each side. Their gowns were pale yellow, and they, too, were wearing masks. One held a thick plastic anesthesia mask in his hand. All eyes were on me.

Then it struck me. *Maybe these are the angels Clay prayed for. All four of them hovering over Leanna, highly trained and ready to do whatever it takes to save her.*

I leaned over the cold metal bedrail and clasped my hand around four of Leanna's puffy fingers, a swollen symbol of her body's struggle. Her head rested back against a pink-and-purple fleece pillowcase sewn by hospital volunteers. Her blonde hair was brushed carefully to the right side. I looked into Leanna's blue-green eyes and saw a look of fear in them I have never seen before. *My baby girl.*

I knew I needed to connect with her, heart and soul, and be quick with God's words. "Leanna, you're in excellent hands. God is with you, and I love you." Because of my mask, all Leanna could see were my eyes, and I imagined them red and puffy from my breakdown in the hall moments before. My eyes spilled my secrets, betraying my motherhood. They punctured the calm comfort I was desperate to give my sweet girl.

Her last words ever spoken, Leanna replied, "I love you too."

My throat tight, I gave her hand a soft squeeze then nodded to the medical team. I turned from the bed and wanted to run from the room, to banish this unbearable scene. Instead, I slowly crossed the gaping expanse of tile as if all of this was in slow motion, then slid through the doorway and into Steve's waiting arms. We stood still, sobbing. For the first time, the thought that Leanna might not come home entered my mind.

Please, God, I pled again. *Please heal her heart. She wants to be your servant. Her work here is not complete! Please don't take her.* I felt I had the upper hand. After all, how on earth could God take someone so young and so dedicated?

After what seemed like days, Dr. Andrews popped through the doorway with an almost buoyant energy. "Everything is done," he announced. "The procedure went well. She will be intubated for a while, but it's likely she won't need an added device to support her heart. Not now, anyway," he added. "Her recovery will take longer than we initially thought. It may be up to a year before her heart heals completely. As for now," he reassured us, "it looks as though Leanna will get through this with no permanent damage."

I collapsed into my chair, head in hands. Steve hovered over me. "Our baby girl made it through," he exclaimed. "Our baby girl made it through! Can we see her?"

"She's medicated so she'll be asleep, but yes, you can go in."

"Come on, Beth." I looked up to see Steve reaching for me.

The lights were dim in Leanna's room. I thought of a photo frame we had at home on our dresser. Baby Leanna, at just eight months old, bald and wearing a plain white romper with a rainbow appliqued on the front. She was perched on her palms and toes as if about to launch into downward-facing dog. The frame was dotted with stars and two dancing clowns asking, "Twinkle, twinkle in your eyes, are you an angel in disguise?"

The room was still, and Leanna's breathing became more relaxed. I tried not to look at the tube coming from her mouth. Her eyes were closed, and I felt a wash of relief seeing her at peace.

Steve took a seat on the far side of the room and pulled out his phone. Clay was already on the way to the hospital and, as we later learned, panicked when he saw Steve's name pop up on the caller ID. "Steve, I'm on my way, just crossing the Sunshine Skyway Bridge."

"Leanna's okay," Steve said. "The intubation went well." For the first time in a week, I saw my husband's shoulders relax.

So why do I still feel afraid?

Clay arrived with huge hugs, and soon after, he and Steve ventured off to the cafeteria to get some coffee. I sat and stared across the room at Leanna then pulled out my phone and looked up Caryn Young's number. I felt compelled to check in with my holistic doctor, desperate for her words of love and support.

I first met Caryn when Leanna was three years old and had come down with a series of lingering colds. Leanna's preschool teacher, Miss Whelma, suggested I take Leanna to a holistic doctor she knew. I didn't know anything about holistic medicine at the time, but Miss Whelma was such a loving and wise spirit, and I knew she had Leanna's best interests at heart, so I decided to give it a try.

———

Approaching her office, it appears to be a typical Sarasota doctor's prac-

tice. But as Leanna and I sit in the waiting area, I take in a large piece of Asian art on the wall, along with a series of framed certificates and diplomas declaring Caryn Young to be a doctor of oriental medicine, an acupuncturist, and an occupational therapist. The scent of Chinese herbs wafts through the space, pleasing my senses. All around, little tables hold crystals of varying shapes and colors, and classical music plays quietly in the background. It is far more relaxing than any doctor's office I've ever been in.

A few minutes later, Caryn strides into the room and greets us. With her brown shoulder-length hair and stylish, crimson-framed glasses, she is the picture of confidence. Her polo shirt and khakis hint at her relaxed, unpretentious nature.

Caryn examines Leanna, looking at her tongue and taking her pulses— as I learned during that visit, we have more than one pulse that can guide a doctor. "Leanna's cold is on the way out. But I think her immune system would benefit from some support to fight off a potential recurrence."

"What kind of support?" I ask.

"There are a few supplements that I would suggest."

Caryn starts describing the various vitamins and herbs and how each supports immune function. It sounds a bit far-fetched to me, but I agree to give them a try.

———

In the end, the cold receded, and while that could have been a coincidence, Caryn's approachable manner and wealth of knowledge brought me back to her, the next time for myself. Under Caryn's teachings and care, my education in holistic medicine began. At first, she gave me little bits of information, which was smart, considering everything I knew about healthcare to that point had a typical Western foundation. She didn't want to scare me off from considering a broader way of approaching life and health. In my prior experience, doctors prescribed antibiotics and other pharmaceuticals, not herbs, acupuncture, and meditation.

I grew amazed at how, by reading my facial expressions or seeing the way I walked into her office, Caryn could tell right away when I was depleted or anxious. Over time, Caryn became not just my doctor, but also a source of quiet, profound support. She even helped me uncover the roots of my ongoing anxieties about life, many of which traced back to my childhood. I'd spent my youth not feeling worthy of my dad's affection and always trying to quell a cruel fear that I wasn't as smart as the other kids. And Caryn helped me begin to face all of it then start to let it go. "Beth, you've got to be with your pain and accept your trials before you can grow beyond them," she once told me. It was no surprise, then, that I reached out to her amid the greatest trial I had ever faced.

I'm so afraid, I texted.

Her response was almost immediate. *Oh, Beth. So much of what happens in this world is beyond our understanding. Faith and trust. Remember that—faith and trust.*

After reading Caryn's message a second time, my phone again lit up. It was a text from Clay.

Girl, you need to stop texting and get some sleep.

I looked across the room to where he was sitting, grinning at me. I laughed and smiled back, then the two of us turned and peered out the window of Leanna's room to watch the sunrise over the shimmering water of Tampa Bay.

Chapter 4

That morning was the last bit of sunshine we saw for nearly a week. Tropical Storm Debby moved in and dominated our weather pattern for the next several days with rain and more rain.

After being in the ICU for four days now, Steve and I were worn down physically and mentally. It had become clear that Leanna would not be home as quickly as we hoped, and the nurses encouraged us to take breaks from our vigil so we wouldn't exhaust ourselves. The hospital staff helped us secure a room at a Ronald McDonald House, which provides free housing for parents of sick children. It was just a few blocks from the hospital, and we would have a private room and bathroom, access to a shared kitchen, and the use of a washer and dryer. It reminded me of a bed and breakfast. The décor was charming with a sunroom, plush sofas, and hardwood floors. For convenience, a buffet spread of bagels and fruit for breakfast or sandwiches for lunch was always laid out in the kitchen.

We got our room the day of the intubation. Clay was still there praying with us and otherwise keeping us company. Rather than drive home that night only to return in the morning, we invited him to spend the night in our corner room on the second floor. The staff provided a rollaway bed. It was close quarters with the extra bed nudged between the wall and our bed, but Clay's presence was comforting. He felt like a lifeline to something bigger.

Clay often led prayer circles at church, but that night, it was just the three of us. Lying there, staring up at the white plaster ceiling surrounded by the glow of a lamp, we spoke our requests aloud. Steve was the first to go and though, in many cases, he is a man of few words, that night was an exception. Steve began with Leanna and asked God to keep her comfortable and free from anxiety; he talked about the doctors and prayed for their skilled hands and expertise; and he prayed for Rogers, that he be kept safe during his travels home from camp.

On and on Steve went, prompting me to wonder at one point whether there would be anything left for me to say. Later, Clay told me he had the same thought. Finally, it was my turn, but I had lost my words. Our daughter had just had a serious medical procedure, and a virus was attacking her heart, but still, my mind went blank; I simply didn't know what to say. Over the last few days, I had gotten through each minute by turning down the volume on my emotions. Now, when I finally had the time and space to truly connect with God—to let it all out—I only felt numb. And I wondered, *Is He even around to hear us?*

I let Clay finish the prayer then drifted into a fitful sleep. Outside, the roaring wind and driving rain persisted as the storm settled in.

The next morning, my first thoughts of the day were dark. *How could I not have prayed?* Then I thought about the hundreds of people who had written on CaringBridge that they were praying for my daughter. Were their appeals enough to cover my lapse?

Anxious to see Leanna, we grabbed bagels from the house kitchen and drove to the hospital. I leaned against the passenger window and stared at the palm trees, which were bent, battered by the wind.

We spent a long morning with a sedated Leanna, getting updates from her nurses on how she had done during the night and talking with the doctors. There was no new information. As I watched her sleep, my stomach twisted with a pang of guilt. Truth be told, I was glad she was asleep. As much as I wanted to talk to Leanna and reassure her, the look of fear I had seen in her eyes before she was intubated haunted me. I did not want her to suffer. I did not want her to be afraid.

"Beth, you look exhausted," Steve said as he kneeled next to my chair. "Why don't you go back and take a nap?"

"Are you sure?"

He nodded. "I'll stay with Leanna. Go get some rest."

Earlier that morning, after we had met with one of the night nurses, Steve had gone out for a run to release some of his anxiety. Maybe some quiet time would help me too. I sighed and took the car keys from his outstretched hand.

Back in our room, I sat on the edge of the bed and let my aloneness sink in. There in my private escape, I released the words I had been holding in.

"God, please don't take her. Please, please, please, *please*, don't take her!" Tears dripped off my chin and onto the carpet as I gasped for breath, my body shaking with fear.

Just breathe, Beth, a voice inside me sounded. *Slow inhale, slow exhale.* My body began to soften, then I scooted back on the bed and lay down on my side, facing the window. Outside, dark clouds hovered, wrapping the day in sadness.

I closed my eyes, but my fluttering heart kept me on edge. Sleep was not happening. The small, solitary room suddenly felt like a gaping wound. Being alone was not good right now. I grabbed my umbrella and drove back to the hospital and ticked down the hours to the end of another dreary day.

That night, instead of going straight back to the Ronald McDonald House, Steve and I stopped at a local restaurant, another attempt to take a break. The thing is, when your child is breathing through a tube in a bed surrounded by so many machines that there is almost no space for you, a break feels like an exercise in futility. Part of you is always in that space. Waiting. Worrying. Wondering. But we had to get out.

We sat at the bar, sipping red wine, and searched for some semblance of normalcy. Steve chattered a bit with the bartender. "I know they're saying he could be the next starter. His college stats were good, but can he handle the pressure of the big leagues? That's what we'll have to see."

I stared at the bottles lining the mirrored wall in front of us. Whiskey, gin, vermouth . . .

"Ma'am?"

"What? Oh, thank you." A waitress placed a plate of food in front of me. What had I ordered? Oh right, salmon.

When Steve and I finally got back to our room, I opened the door to find a note on the floor. A small white piece of paper read, "You were supposed to vacuum the hall today." Apparently, families were meant to pitch in with the household chores.

I turned to Steve. "You have *got* to be kidding me."

Steve took the paper, shook his head, and crushed it into a tight ball. He turned toward the bathroom, tossing the note in the trashcan as he passed.

———

I looked at the face of my sweet daughter in repose. As I spoke to her, I wondered whether my words got snagged in all the tubes or made it to my girl's heart.

"Hi, sweetheart. So many people are asking about you and praying for you. I hope you can feel that."

I looked at the heart rate monitor above Leanna's bed and watched as the red numbers ticked slowly down, then settled. *Beep, beep, beep.* The steady electronic echo of my daughter's heartbeat signaled once again to me that Leanna could hear us.

It was hard to find her hand among the tubes littering her bed, and I did not want to disturb any of them. Instead, I wrapped my arms around myself and rubbed the soft cotton of the green sweatshirt Leanna had bought from Marshall University. I had put it on to feel her close.

My phone vibrated in my lap. Another of Leanna's friends was texting, asking when they might be able to visit. With some reluctance, I played the role of the gatekeeper. Steve and I were flooded with requests to see Leanna, and all I wanted to do was protect her. Leanna's state was so fragile that I worried about so many people coming to her room. It was apparent that even sedated, Leanna had some awareness of what was going on around her, and I worried that all that traffic would exhaust her. And then there was the risk of transmitting germs.

We made an exception for Josh, though. Soon after the intubation, we decided to let him see Leanna. As with the few others we allowed to visit, we warned him. "Josh, you're used to Leanna looking a certain way. Keep that Leanna in mind when you see her. She's still beautiful, but she'll probably just lie there with her eyes closed most of the time."

Josh, who had been in the Adirondacks on a trip to his family's cabin, had been texting Leanna—and us—like crazy. He was delighted when we granted his request to see her. Leanna's nurses, always attentive, switched into "spa mode," washing her hair and painting her nails bright pink because they wanted her to look her best for her boyfriend's visit.

"Hey, Leanna." Josh hovered near the foot of her bed. He looked up at Steve and me, eyebrows raised in a question. He combed through his red hair, not sure what to do. As he considered her, I could see the blood flush into his cheeks. Steve nodded and motioned him closer to Leanna. Josh took a step forward. "I, um, I brought you this," he said, holding up a small plush German shepherd. "His name's Lucky, cause, you know, I figured you could use some right now." Josh turned to me.

"We'll put Lucky high on this shelf where he can watch over Leanna," I said, nudging aside several cards to make room.

Josh fidgeted for a moment, unsure of what to say to someone who could not respond, but as he stood there looking down at Leanna, he somehow rose to the occasion. He described his family's vacation and the long car ride, then talked about some songs he was putting on a playlist for Leanna. "I bet you can't wait for the Coldplay concert. Only a week to go!" he said. "It's gonna be amazing, Leanna, so, you've got to get better for that, okay? No pressure or anything," he smiled. As Josh spoke, Leanna's vital signs stabilized, the sound of her heart rate settling again to a steady procession of beeps.

After his visit, Josh had a dream in which Leanna was in a hospital bed, fully conscious, smiling down at a little red-headed baby in her arms. "I think it means she's going to be okay!" he told me.

I, myself, had imagined the path of my daughter's life as a wife and mother.

Leanna had grown up going to church. She joyfully went to Sunday school and took part in youth outings and the kids' pageants. At age eight she played the Virgin Mary in the Christmas pageant, kneeling in the hay, marveling at her baby boy. For his role, Rogers brought the house down the year he sauntered down the aisle in a life-sized camel costume that he had made himself. But I will never forget that image of Leanna wrapped in a simple blue robe made from an old bedsheet. Looking at her then, somehow the child Leanna disappeared, and in her soft facial features, a young mother came into light.

I glanced back at Leanna and thought again of the diamond necklace Steve had given me with the intention that it would one day be Leanna's when she became a mother.

Please God…

———

Prayer with Clay and the hospital chaplain, David Pitt, helped to guide us through what felt like endless days in the hospital sitting with

Leanna, meeting with doctors, pacing the halls, and taking the elevators up and down to the cafeteria, the waiting room, the parking garage. Each time we boarded the elevator and pressed a number, a cheerful child's voice announced, "Going up!" or "Going down."

Meanwhile, I continued to post on CaringBridge. It became a nightly ritual after we returned to our room at the Ronald McDonald House. I was astounded at the number of people from our church and the larger community who were engaged with Leanna's plight and agonized by her illness. At one point, I invited them to pray with me, telling Steve, "If we can focus everyone's energy on a single message, that has to be powerful, right?"

> *Dear Heavenly Father, we come to you in prayer and ask for your blessings on Leanna. Surround her with your love and give her strength. Lord, guide her doctors and nurses, steadying their hands and their minds...*

Many friends and family members had begun to show up at the hospital, keeping vigil in the frigid waiting room. Greg Simmons often visited after his own long days at work, driving halfway across the state from Orlando Regional Medical Center, and helped translate all the medical jargon into plain English. We were surrounded by voices. Medical staff issued a string of orders, updates, and prognoses. The crowd in the waiting room murmured prayers and support. Even the elevator chirped a chipper message. Yet Leanna's voice, the one we so longed to hear, had been silenced.

———

On Monday morning, after a week in the hospital, the staff arranged for us to be transferred to another Ronald McDonald House, this one on hospital grounds. It was designed for families of patients in the ICU and didn't ask overwhelmed parents to do chores. The tiny, modest room was more modern but similar in amenities to the one we had just come from—a queen bed, a bathroom, a dresser with a television. We spent a few minutes getting settled, then left for Leanna's room to check on her.

As Steve and I walked by the nurses' station, Leanna's head nurse popped up and stopped us. "I'm glad you're here. The doctors would like to talk to you about the next steps."

Next steps?

"I'll take you back to see them," she said, her tone solemn.

"Okay?" I replied, and we followed her down the hall to a small conference room where Leanna's team of doctors convened.

Steve grabbed my hand. We took a deep breath and sat in the hard metal chairs. Leanna's surgeon, Dr. Simon, did all the talking.

"I'm afraid that Leanna's heart is struggling to do its job. At this point, her circulation is not what we'd like it to be. To help her, we need to install a heart pump called a left ventricle assist device, or L-VAD. It will give her heart a boost and help it to pump more effectively."

I heard Steve let out a long sigh. I swallowed hard then braced myself.

"To install this L-VAD, do you have to open her chest?" I asked, afraid of the answer.

"Yes," he said, "we have to open her sternum."

I turned to Steve, whose red eyes glistened, then glanced back at the surgeon who sat motionless and expressionless, looking at me. I dropped my head into my hands as tears erupted.

The following morning, at 8:30 a.m., a team of medical staff wheeled our daughter off to the operating room while we sat with Chris, Maureen, and a host of others, though their faces and well wishes were a blur. The lives of everyone in our circle of friends and family came to a standstill that morning. Our friends from home held a candlelit vigil at church and messages poured into the CaringBridge site:

We have flooded the throne room of heaven with prayer for Leanna as she is in surgery. We are praying for her safety, protection, and healing through this procedure. We pray for the surgeons and OR teams to work with God-given skill and precision. And for Leanna to come through this, be at peace, and for her recovery time to make her healed and strong again. We are praying for you as well that our loving God would rain His mercy down on you, and surround you, fill, and saturate you with His peace and assurance. He is in control, and He loves Leanna.

I also posted a message to Leanna on CaringBridge:

My sweet angel, Leanna . . . God is holding you in the palm of His hand, protecting you and giving you strength. Your friends and family are praying for you incessantly. You are loved by many as you are so very, very special . . . I love you. You are my hero.

Three hours into the surgery, a woman from the OR team opened the door to the waiting room. Wearing blue scrubs and a surgical cap, she delivered an update: "We are about halfway through the procedure. Everything is going as expected. We will continue to keep you informed of our progress."

Around 2:00 p.m. that afternoon, Leanna was out of surgery. Steve and I met with the surgeon and cardiologist. "The placement of the L-VAD went as well as it possibly could have," said Dr. Simon, "but as an extra precaution, Leanna will be kept in the OR so that she can be closely monitored."

We were pacing in circles outside Leanna's room when they finally rolled her back in, a team of scrub-clad figures maneuvering her bed, along with the growing number of machines connected to our daughter. As they got everything situated, Steve and I walked in and flanked Leanna's bed, trying our best to trust that the L-VAD was going to save our daughter's life. Silently I prayed, *Lord, please . . . please let this device do its job so we can have our sweet Leanna back home with us.*

After sitting in a windowless waiting room for hours upon hours, Steve welcomed a view of the outside world. As he walked over to the window in Leanna's room, he noticed a swirling mixture of white clouds and blue skies. "Hey, look outside!" he said, offering a hopeful smile, "the storm has cleared."

Then Dr. Everett motioned us to join him in the hall. "As we said earlier, everything went as expected. Leanna's liver, kidneys, and lungs are now getting the oxygen-rich blood supply they need, thanks to the pump. Still . . ." he paused. "We're putting Leanna on the list for a heart transplant. She's stable now, and we may never get to the point where she needs it, but it's a long list, and due to the delicate nature of Leanna's condition, we think it's a sensible move."

Steve and I nodded, unable to process the full impact of the doctor's words.

———

Soon after Leanna's surgery, Rogers flew home from New York with his friend, Eli, who attended the camp with him, and Eli's parents. Steve and I were deeply disappointed to miss his performance, but Rogers knew we would have been there if we could. By now, it was evident that his sister was fighting far more than just the flu.

Steve met Rogers at the Sarasota airport. When Melissa, Eli's mother, delivered Rogers to Steve, she grabbed Rogers's bag off the luggage belt and insisted on taking his dirty clothes home with her to wash them herself. It was one more little act of kindness that, throughout our ordeal, added up to help us feel loved and supported in a way we had never experienced before.

From the airport, Steve drove straight to the hospital, but Rogers had caught a bad cold in New York and was coughing and sneezing. As much as we wanted him to see his sister, it was not wise to bring him to Leanna's room. My father had come down from Virginia, and he, Rogers, Steve, and I gathered for dinner at an Italian restaurant a few miles from the hospital. Rogers was in such a sorry state of illness that after our meal, Steve took him to the ER, where they gave him an antibiotic. Rogers spent the next few days quarantined in our room at the Ronald McDonald House.

Finally, with the antibiotic fully in his system, Rogers was deemed well enough to see Leanna. After a quick breakfast in the communal kitchen at the Ronald McDonald House, we walked our familiar path to the intensive care unit. When we got there, Dr. Everett was leaving Leanna's room.

"You must be the famous Rogers," he said, reaching to shake Rogers's hand. "Hi, I'm Dr. Everett, one of Leanna's doctors."

Rogers, always a confident kid, returned the shake with a smile. "It's nice to meet you."

"Rogers, if it's okay with your mom and dad, I'd like to talk to you for a few minutes before you go in to see your sister." Steve and I nodded. We trusted Dr. Everett.

"Rogers, I just wanted to prepare you for what you're going to see," he said when they sat. "Your sister is in very good hands, but she's dealing with a lot. We've had to put a tube in her throat, to help her breathe, and we've installed a pump in her heart to help circulate her blood. I know your mom and dad have told you all of this."

Rogers nodded, his face blank.

"So each of those devices is hooked to a machine. And there are other machines around Leanna's bed monitoring her heart rate, her blood oxygen level, and so on. There's a lot of beeping, and some nurses will be coming in and out to check on things. And your sister is asleep.

It's unlikely she will wake up while you're in there because we're keeping her relaxed so her body doesn't have to work harder than it needs to. Do you understand?"

Rogers again nodded.

"Do you have any questions for me?"

Rogers shook his head.

"Okay, well if you think of any, I'm here, okay? I'm always happy to talk to you."

"Thank you," Rogers said, and the two rose and turned to Steve and me.

When we finally went into her room, Rogers walked slowly up to Leanna's bed, his eyes fixed on her face.

"Hey, Leanna. It's me. I'm finally here. I'm sorry you missed my show in New York because, you know, I crushed it," he smiled, prompting a smile from Steve and me. "You've gotta get better because there's so much stuff I have to tell you, okay? And there are some really cool music videos I want to show you." I felt the muscles of my throat constrict as I looked across the room at my children.

Suddenly, in my mind's eye, we are on a family trip to Africa and Rogers is begging Leanna to borrow the new camera we'd given her for her birthday.

———

"I said no, Rogers," she implores.

"Come onnnn! Pleeeeese?! I'll be careful with it, I promise."

For two years, Steve and I had talked about taking the family on a wildlife safari in Africa. In 2011, he said to me, "The kids are old enough now; let's do it!" Steve and I were giddy with excitement when we walked into Leanna's bedroom to tell her.

"Leanna, guess what's happening next July?" we tease.

"Ohh, what?" she asks, eyes sparkling, glancing up from her phone.

"We're going to Africa! We're going on safari!"

"Are you kidding me?" she beams with excitement. Then, it seems, clouds settle in her eyes. "When in July? Do you have the dates?"

"I can get back to you with the exact dates," I reply, "but, it's the second week in July."

Her shoulders slump. "But, but . . . that means I'll miss the Montreat Youth Conference," she says, eyes falling back to her phone.

Steve and I sit down on her bed. We are talking Africa—a trip of a lifetime! Still, we know how important the conference is to Leanna and want to support her. "We can work all of that out. We'll find a way to get you to Montreat on time. I promise," Steve assures her.

Leanna's smile returns as she looks up from her phone. "Really? You mean it?"

———

Early the following July, we fly to Johannesburg, then take a connecting flight to Cape Town and rent an apartment near the Victoria & Alfred Waterfront. Enjoying blue skies and cooler temperatures, we drive down the coast to the Cape of Good Hope at the southwestern tip of Africa. Mountains surround us, and turquoise water laps at our feet. We also take a ferry to Robben Island to see the musty pale-green jail cell where Nelson Mandela was confined for eighteen years.

After a few days of sightseeing, we are off to meet the rest of our tour group, led by our friends Michael and Terri Klauber, at the legendary Victoria Falls. Leaving the urban oasis of Cape Town, as we gaze out the windows of our car on our way to the airport, we see the landscape change dramatically. Along the highway, dotting the countryside as far as the eye can see are shanty towns pieced together with plywood and corrugated metal. Tall poles

holding up power lines lean against other poles, the whole arrangement look-
ing as if a strong gust of wind could collapse it all. How can people live in
these conditions? *I wonder.*

Leanna, too, is shaken by what we see. She peppers me with questions.
"What about school, Mom? Do they go to school? Do they have enough
clothes and food?"

"I don't know, sweetheart," I say as we roll on.

Later that day, when we arrive at our hotel in Victoria Falls, the first
activity on the agenda is to see the falls while it is still daylight. Draped in
dark-green ponchos designed to keep the mist from soaking our clothes, we
walk the path along the edge of the gorge to get a glimpse of one of the largest
waterfalls in the world. We stand in awe of the constant rainbow formed
as the sunlight hits the mist from the falls. To our right is the Victoria Falls
Bridge, which crosses the Zambezi River. It is all Steve and I can do to quell
Rogers's desire to bungee jump off of the bridge. Despite his assurances that it
is "perfectly safe," we decline.

A few more days into our trip, we fly to the Londolozi Game Reserve.
"Londolozi" is a Zulu word for "protector of all living things," and the focus
of this magical place is on conserving the land and protecting the wildlife. It
is breathtaking. Even in winter, there are lush trees along the river and open
plains of tall golden grasses, along with lions, leopards, elephants, and a trea-
sure of birds, large and small, of every kind and color. There are wild dogs,
hyenas, and huge rhinos with their weathered grey skin. Leanna photographs
them all. Her camera constantly clicking, Leanna seems to have a natural
eye. Her photo of a leopard's arrow-sharp stare straight into the camera, now
framed and hung on our wall, takes me back to that very moment every time.

"Mom," she tells me one night while we listen to the lions roaring in the
distance, the vibrations causing tremors in the ground for miles. "This is a
holy place. It really is a sanctuary."

As we look out into the cool air from our room that evening, blankets
wrapped around our shoulders, I feel a deep connection with my daughter as

we absorb the truth of her statement. This is hallowed ground, and we are so lucky to be sharing it with one another and with these incredible people and animals. It is a moment that holds both the present and infinity, as though our entire lives—past, present, and future—are cradled together. The place inspires all of us, but something deep within Leanna is especially stirred.

By the third night on safari, Leanna has fallen in love with this most enchanting and exotic place.

"Hey Mom, guess what?" Leanna says, leaning her head on my shoulder after dinner in the boma, a protected outdoor dining area, "I'm going to come back here for my honeymoon." I smile at the thought of this as the Milky Way hovers above us.

Eventually, during the trip, Leanna relents and lets Rogers borrow her camera. "Five minutes!" she declares. "Not a second more."

"Thanks," he says, snatching it from her hands.

"Rogers be careful with your sister's camera. It's a delicate piece of equipment," I admonish.

"I know, Mom." Rogers mutters something to his sister and they laugh.

———

And now there he was, Leanna's baby brother standing over her. His voice was hushed, and I could no longer hear what he was saying. His earnestness broke my heart. He masked his pain, as Rogers does so well, in humor. At one point, he grinned and looked over at us, and I could just tell that in their way, they were once again sharing an inside joke about Mom and Dad. It warmed my heart to see them together again.

Somehow, in the insanity of our situation, we began to develop a kind of rhythm. The night nurses at the hospital ended their shift at 7:00 a.m. Every morning, Steve and I would be in Leanna's room by 6:45 a.m. to learn how she'd done during the night. We listened in as the nurses ending their shift ran through a list of updates with those coming on duty. After we were caught up on the latest, Steve would go out for a run then head back to the Ronald McDonald House to shower and return in time for the doctors' 9:00 a.m. rounds. I went out for walks, trying desperately to connect with the sustaining peace nature had always offered me.

At rounds, a swarm of doctors and nurses gathered in the hall outside Leanna's door and compared notes on her condition. Specialists and interns hunched over their laptops settled on tall rolling carts, combing through the overnight data from her multiple machines. Test results were analyzed, medications adjusted, additional tests scheduled. Every symptom was noted, every option explored. Some of it made sense to me; much didn't, but the staff did their best to explain, and we leaned on Steve's friend Greg to fill the gaps.

As the minutes and hours ticked by, it was apparent that everyone was doing all they could. Now it seemed like a waiting game. Would the doctors be able to fix Leanna's heart, or would they have to implant a new one? And if her heart couldn't be healed, would another be available in time?

My conversations with God had deteriorated into ragged begging. *Please,* I thought over and over. *Please, please, please.*

In this place of darkness, we needed a miracle.

Chapter 5

"You should go."

"What?"

"To the concert. You should go."

"Huh?" I turned to Steve. Sitting there, staring at Leanna, my mind was wandering down the random alleys and byways of my memory. Before Steve interrupted, Leanna was a crawling baby. Vidisha, a friend from Lamaze class, was expecting again. We sat one day watching her son, Chetan, and Leanna play. Out of nowhere, little Chetan, eyes sparkling, leaned over and planted a kiss on Leanna's forehead. Vidisha and I erupted into laughter. "Her first kiss from a boy!" I exclaimed.

"We'll have to remind them of that when it's time for senior prom," Vidisha joked.

Senior prom, I thought looking at Leanna, asleep in the hospital bed. *Somehow it seems even farther away now than it did back then.*

"Beth?" Steve persisted.

I sighed. "Sorry, I was just—What did you say?"

"The Coldplay concert. I think you should go. I'll stay here with Leanna."

"I don't know, Steve. I don't think I can. It just doesn't feel right." Months before, Leanna and Christina had learned that Coldplay was coming to Tampa on June 28. It was one of Leanna's favorite bands. We ended up getting tickets for the whole family, along with Christina and her family, and the two girls had been talking about it ever since.

Music has always had a special place in our family's life—together and as individuals. Growing up, I played the oboe in my school's concert band and youth symphony then attended music camps at East Carolina University. One of my proudest moments as a kid was making it into the regional band, a rare accomplishment for a seventh-grader. I was an insecure kid, and music was one place I could shine.

Music also transported me. Throughout my childhood, popular songs were a shield from the turmoil around me. They were pieces of happiness, little kingdoms in a time capsule, places I still revisit every time certain songs come on the radio. When I hear Steely Dan play "Do It Again" or John Denver sing "Take Me Home, Country Roads," I'm in 1972 all over again. I am back in my bedroom, with the antique dresser and its hidden drawer where I stashed notes from boys, with my 8-track tape player, playing solitaire or slinging my purple yo-yo. That was my place of escape.

As a teen, the Jackson Browne song, "Hold On, Hold Out," left an imprint on my soul. I would sit and listen to that song, the piano pounding out the melody, with drums, organ, synthesizer, and Jackson Browne and his female backup singer belting it out, telling me to just hold on and be strong. Somehow, it made me realize there was real substance beneath the surface of daily life. I hungered for meaning in life and looked for it in songs.

For his part, Steve listens to thousands of albums of nearly every genre. When Leanna was born, he brought a Pat Metheny cassette tape to the hospital to smooth the edges of my nerves during labor and delivery. When she was just six months old, the three of us flew to Michigan for a music festival. We spread out blankets on the sweeping green lawn and snuggled with our baby girl as jazz notes rose into the blue sky. "She's got long fingers," Steve had said as he held his newborn daughter's tiny hand in his. "She's going to be a piano player." Steve was right. Leanna played both the piano and guitar.

I looked at those slender fingers, much longer now, resting on her belly, folded gently one on top of the other over the hospital blanket. Rogers, too, plays the piano and guitar. Their packed schedules often had them in different places at different times, sometimes seeing each other only at meals and church, but they always made time here and there to share new favorite songs and bands like little treasures they'd found.

Music was a way we bonded as a family; a language we spoke. When Rogers and Leanna were little, we spent hours listening and singing along to the soundtracks from "Brother Bear" and "Tarzan," the kids spinning around, dancing. In the car, shuttling from place to place, the kids took turns playing their favorite tunes.

Music in general, but Coldplay in particular, had helped me connect with Leanna at a time when I felt her slipping away. The year before, at age fifteen, she had started dating Josh—a sweet rower who was crazy about Leanna and never seemed to leave her side. During that time, she spent endless hours on social media and rarely practiced the piano anymore. She'd sprawl out on her bed, papers and clothes strewn all over, posting and texting and Skyping with Josh. As friends became her world, I longed for ways to stay close. One ordinary morning, as I was driving the kids to their schools in the dark and trying to work out the logistics of that afternoon, a song came on the radio.

"Mom, turn it up," Leanna had said, leaning forward in her seat. "It's Coldplay!" Hypnotic strains filled the car. "It's called 'Fix You.' Chris Martin, the singer, wrote it for his wife after her father died."

"He's married to that actress," Rogers chimed in from the back seat.

"Gwyneth Paltrow," Leanna confirmed.

I remembered listening to the singer's high tenor and the plain, almost despairing words supported by simple organ chords behind him. The song struck me just as "Hold On, Hold Out" had when I first heard it some thirty years before. In those brief minutes, I felt connected with the kids in a way I had not in a long time. It was the kind of moment that when it is happening you don't know how important it is, but later, you realize it is one of the biggest scenes of your life.

"Beth?" Steve nudged. "Did I lose you again?"

"Sorry," I said. "Maybe I will go to the concert. Are you sure you wouldn't mind?"

"Absolutely. And hey, why don't you take Clay with you? He can use my ticket."

"Clay?"

"Yeah, he's been so supportive. He's here at the hospital most of the time. I'm sure he could use a break."

"Yeah," I nodded, thinking it would be good for Rogers to have at least one of his family members there with him, and Rogers always connected with the big kid in Clay as well. In a couple of weeks, Rogers and Clay would be heading to Montreat, the youth conference that meant so much to Leanna.

Understandably, we were devoting most of our time and energy to Leanna, but it would be nice to share a special night with our son. Rogers and I could give Leanna a full recap of the concert when she recovered, and I could at least get her a t-shirt. The next time Coldplay came through town, we would make a point to see them as a family.

———

"They said something might happen!" Christina exclaimed to our little group gathered in front of the merchandise stands. Leanna's best friend was doing everything she could to make it up to her friend for missing the concert they had been dreaming of for years. She and some of her family who joined her at the concert were all sporting homemade neon-green t-shirts with "#TeamLeanna" and "Fix You" emblazoned across the back.

"I have this idea!" Christina had told me a few days before. "I wonder if I could get Chris Martin to, like, make a little video with the song 'Fix You' and dedicate it to Leanna." Though the idea seemed far-fetched, Christina wrote a letter to the band and posted it all over social media with the #TeamLeanna hashtag. She even started a Facebook page called A Letter to Coldplay. A few days later, Christina got an email from the band's fan liaison, gently declining her request. It was standard language. "I'm sorry we can't honor your request . . . If we did it for you, we'd have to do it for everyone."

A dedicated friend, Christina persisted. She scoured the internet for ways to connect with anyone close to the band. One tiny toehold led to another, then another, until one of the contacts was able to get Christina past the fan liaison and in touch with the band's manager.

As our group huddled together outside the concert hall, Christina filled us in on her efforts to get Coldplay to somehow acknowledge Leanna. "The manager said if something happens, and he couldn't promise it, but that if it did, it would be subtle—something only our group would notice." Rogers, Clay, our former sitter, Jenn, and Christina and her gang came in close, hands clasped, and prayed that the band would somehow mention Leanna. There was just something magical about the setup—Leanna's love of Coldplay, Christina's persistence, my moment with Leanna and Rogers in the car listening to "Fix You," and people bustling and humming all around us.

After scanning our tickets, the event staff handed us electronic bracelets. As the crowd milled about, tiny waves of lights glowed all around us. We were on the verge of something, I could feel it. Maybe it was the miracle we needed.

After a second huddled prayer, I sent everyone on to their seats. "I'm going to get a t-shirt for Leanna," I said. "I'll be right behind you," I called out after them.

The merchandise line was packed, and as I turned back toward the cue, I felt my elbow graze something.

"Whoa!" a man exclaimed, jumping back, foamy liquid spilling everywhere. He was lean with a baseball cap and the type of scraggly facial hair popular with younger guys. He frowned as both our eyes fell on his plastic beer cup, now half empty.

"I'm so sorry," I said. "Can I . . ." I was about to offer to buy him another but instead erupted into tears.

"Oh, hey," he said, his face softening. "It's okay, really. Accidents happen. It's not a big deal."

"I'm sorry," I repeated, wiping at my cheeks. "It's . . . It's my daughter. She's been in the hospital for over a week. We don't know if she's going to be okay."

"Oh, my gosh. I'm so sorry," he said. I looked up at this stranger staring straight into my eyes and for a moment, the scene around us faded. We looked at one another and in that split-second of pure presence, something passed between us, and it hit me. *People care. They care about us, and they care about Leanna. Total strangers. We are all connected.*

What was happening with Leanna mattered, and not just to our radius of family and friends. Hundreds of people were now following Leanna's struggle through our CaringBridge page and praying for her to be healed. Many of them only knew her by her story.

The volume rose again on the scene around us. "Thank you," I said to the man. We looked at each other for another long moment, then I turned toward the t-shirt stand, and he disappeared into the crowd.

Finally, I made it to my seat and settled in next to Rogers, on a lower level just to the front and right of the stage. The stadium was packed to the rafters. The lights came down, and all around us, the crowd began to cheer. Our bracelets pulsed a rainbow of colors as the band started to play.

We sat through song after song. The music was electrifying, but I was distracted, sitting upright on the edge of my seat, waiting and watching for any sign that might be for us. Finally, a chorus of cheers settled after one song concluded, then a spotlight illuminated the lanky, red-shirted form of Chris Martin. He sat in the middle of the stage at an upright piano painted with starbursts, swirls, and hearts. Suddenly, I recognized the haunting chords that signaled the beginning of "Fix You." From the corner of my eye, I saw Rogers perk up. All around us, the crowd began to sway and sing along. My body tensed. Then, in the brief interlude after the first stanza, Chris Martin leaned into the microphone and with crystal clarity said, "We're singing this for our friend, Leanna."

For a second, I froze, mouth open. Rogers and I looked at each other; then, in a flash we were on our feet, hugging and screaming and jumping up and down. "Oh my gosh! Oh my gosh!" we shouted, tears and laughter, emoting all at once.

The tempo picked up and the lead singer grabbed a discarded gray t-shirt and began jumping and twirling it over his head as he made his way to center stage. Throwing the shirt back toward the band, he ran forward onto a part of the stage that extended into the crowd, and as the music rose to a crescendo, jumped into the air once, twice, then three times, throwing his arms up and legs back. Around us, twenty thousand people were singing with one voice, our bracelets flashing as Chris Martin placed his hand over his heart and patted his chest, then pointed at us. Rogers, Clay, Jenn, and I continued to jump and scream, and I swore I could hear Christina's squeals from across the stadium. At that moment, it was as if all those people, everyone from CaringBridge, our families, our friends, and everyone from church were united by a single powerful force, sharing this song about the deepest kind of loss, finding the light, and getting home.

You did this, Leanna. You made this happen, I thought. *You brought us all together.*

Finally, the song began to slow, and Chris Martin returned to the piano. As "Fix You" drew to a close, he stood with his right hand playing the final notes, his left hand resting over his heart. His loving salute to Leanna. Chills broke out all over my body as my eyes filled with tears.

When I returned to the Ronald McDonald House that night, I was dying to tell Steve what happened, but he was fast asleep after another long night at the hospital. I didn't dare wake him.

———

I rose the next morning with a spark I had not felt since Leanna had first become ill. I could not wait to share what had happened with the team. I strode into the hospital still buzzing with electricity from the night before. I had been feeling useless through this entire ordeal, and I *finally* had something meaningful to share—something uplifting for everyone. What happened was a sign from God that Leanna was going to be healed. She would be okay. I just *knew* it.

"Guess what?" I said as the doctors and nurses gathered with their computers for their 9:00 a.m. consultation. "You won't believe what happened last night at the Coldplay concert." A choir of blank stares met me in response.

Okay, fine then. I'll wait until after the meeting to tell them. Yet by then, the enthusiasm that had powered me through the night fizzled. What had happened the night before had been nothing short of magic, but the medical team's flat, somber tones crashed me back to the real world with the ferocity of a car wreck. Leanna was not fixed, and she had a very long way to go if she was ever going to make it back home.

"What was it you wanted to say?" the intensivist asked.

"Oh, nothing. Never mind."

Chapter 6

"The L-VAD pump isn't producing the results we'd hoped for," Dr. Everett said. "Leanna's heart is just too weak. We need a stronger solution."

The following day, we were back in the conference room, seated around a table as if we were going over a corporation's quarterly reports. Everything felt cold and hard, from the laminate table and metal chairs to the words from the doctors' mouths. They were probably as warm and kind as they could be given the situation, but even Dr. Everett's sunny disposition seemed to have darkened a bit, like a dimmer switch nudged downward.

"What's the solution?" Steve asked, placing his hand on my knee.

"We want to install a new machine called an ECMO, for extracorporeal membrane oxygenation." I winced, my heart sinking. Though I had no real clue what he was talking about, it was clear things were going in the wrong direction. The doctor continued, "It would pump the blood outside the body to an artificial lung, essentially, that would clean Leanna's blood and fill it with oxygen. It wouldn't fix her heart, but it would take over and allow her heart to rest and hopefully get stronger."

"Another surgery?" I asked.

"Yes," he nodded. "We'll need to remove the L-VAD and install the bypass system."

I heard Steve take a deep breath. We looked at one another, our exhausted eyes exchanging volumes. *How much more of this can we take? I asked silently. How much more can Leanna take?*

Steve's gaze was still, like a lake on a windless day. *One step at a time,* it said. He gave my knee a light squeeze. I nodded. Steve turned back to the doctors. "Okay," he said.

Before I knew it, they were once again wheeling our daughter off behind the heavy steel doors. Clay and our ever-growing band of supporters sat vigil with us again. I stared at the floor for what seemed like an hour, then looked up at the clock to find only minutes had passed. Hospital time. It was like a science fiction movie with time warps where space and time twisted into total distortion. What felt like three days was only one, yet the gap between life and death could be measured by seconds. We waited and waited.

Rrrrr, my phone buzzed. A text from Rogers.

Any news?

Not yet, I texted back. *It will probably be a while yet. I'll let you know as soon as she's out.*

Okay, thanks.

———

Where was Rogers in all this? It was hard to tell, or maybe I was just too distracted to notice. We tried to create some sense of normalcy for him, shuttling him to and from friends' houses or summer camp programs. When he wasn't eating or staying overnight with a friend, he was going out to dinner with us and staying at the Ronald McDonald house.

"How were the kids today?" I'd ask when I picked him up from Florida Studio Theatre where he helped with the youth program.

"They were good. You know." He'd offer a smile then turn back to his phone.

In those moments, I did my best to connect, but my entire being was anchored to Leanna. Everything outside the hospital seemed to exist in a flat, two-dimensional plane, leaving Rogers with a cardboard cutout of a mom. Everyday topics felt foreign—the weather and the news and everything else beyond what was happening in the cardiovascular ICU was a language I struggled to speak.

Yet overall, Rogers seemed his usual self, so light and charismatic that it was hard to know what was really going on inside him. Still quick with a smile or a joke, he seemed to be oblivious to what was happening in her hospital bed. I couldn't tell if he understood how serious things were, or if that was just his way of dealing.

———

"Good news." Steve and I looked up to see Dr. Simon standing over us. "The procedure was successful," he proclaimed with a muted smile.

We returned to Leanna's room to find the ECMO console and monitor crowded into a corner with its collection of tubes. I stared, mesmerized, at a red tube. *That's Leanna's blood.*

An attendant perched on a chair next to the machine, watching the electronic display panel and every so often, adjusting a dial. The ECMO was so complex and its function so critical that from then on, nurses took shifts sitting guard, monitoring its function 24/7.

———

"Beth, Steve . . ." I was beginning to dread that prologue. It was now a few days after they hooked Leanna up to the ECMO. Dr. Simon peered at us from across the table once more. "Leanna's kidneys are struggling. Given what's happening with her heart, that's not surprising, but it means we're going to have to start dialysis."

This time, Steve and I don't bother looking at each other. Another device. Each moment it is becoming clearer that every major organ in our daughter's body is being supported by some beeping machine.

Most of our time at the hospital was just sitting around waiting for some aspect of Leanna's health to improve and praying for change that wasn't for the worse. For me, the endless hours offered time to examine everything I knew about my daughter, who seemed almost like a stranger splayed on the unforgiving bed, nestled by machines and cords. Once again, I recalled the immediate joy I felt in keeping her safe as a child. Now, all the prayers I could muster, all the medical equipment I could offer access to, all the expertise I could afford to her, none of it mattered and nothing seemed to help. I could hope and pray all I wanted. She was slipping.

Maybe it was the feeling of helplessness, more than the waiting itself, that was so exhausting. We were at the mercy of . . . *something*. We had no idea what larger picture was unfolding before us. Instead, we felt the unending march of minutes and hours that were either leading our daughter closer to or farther away from us. There was no way to know which.

Steve and I were hitting a low point, and the nurses could tell. "Why don't you get out more?" Carrie, one of Leanna's regular nurses, had just finished adjusting Leanna's IV. "I know it's hard to leave her, but we're here. Take some time for yourselves. Take walks, get fresh air, clear your minds." She laid a loving hand on my tense shoulder. "It's important."

Nearly every night, after talking with the night shift nurses as they came on duty, Steve and I forced ourselves to go out for dinner. I felt guilty leaving Leanna even for an hour or two, but I was grateful that in our absence, Steve's father, Wally, and his wife, Marcia, would fill in for us, carefully covering themselves with gowns and masks to be in her room.

At dinner, Steve and I often sat without speaking more than a few words to one another. We typically chose a place with a bar so we could be side by side in silence, instead of having to sit across from each other and confront what was happening. The server would glide over, smile, and ask the usual question. "How are you two doing tonight?"

Sometimes, we lied and said we were fine. Other nights, we simply said, "We're here because our daughter is in the hospital."

Despite Steve's reserved nature, when he meets a person with an accent, without realizing it, he matches their manner of speaking. One night, we were sitting, a long silence suspended between us as we drank our glass of wine, cell phones visible and ready in case the hospital called. We tried to find something to talk about other than Leanna but quickly abandoned the attempt and instead lapsed into silence. Then a server pulled up, greeting us with a light Southern drawl. "Hey, y'all. I see you've already gotten squared away with drinks. What can I get you for dinner?"

"Kain-tucky?" Steve asked with his own made-up drawl.

The server laughed. "Good ear!"

I watched as the two of them began to chatter away. Steve was a rock. A man so much more reliable and so much kinder than my own father had been.

———

I'd spent the early part of my life trying to earn my dad's attention, and it was a mission that seemed doomed from the start. My dad was a banker, a real bigwig in our town. Everyone knew him. Everyone respected him. For us kids though, he was a distant figure.

A charismatic man, Dad lived large and spent money easily on nice suits, a big house, cars—anything that would show others he'd made it. But when it came to his family, his big bright light dimmed to a flicker. He was never interested in spending time with his kids, and though he made plenty of money, I barely had the clothes I needed for school. When Dad left us, Mom struggled to make ends meet for the four kids who yearned after him. I resolved to earn a stable career that would make my dad proud.

By 1989, I was twenty-five years old, slogging away as a loan officer at a bank. It had been just over two years since I'd moved to Florida from Virginia, where I'd grown up. My job as a commercial banker allowed me to support myself, but life felt flat. I'd gotten on this path because following in my dad's footsteps seemed like a way to finally gain his approval. Because I had grown up longing for a connection with him, when it was time for college, finance seemed like a solid choice. I trusted that banking would lead me somewhere worthy, and even though I learned a lot, it was not me. Still, in an unexpected way, choosing the wrong career path ended up changing my life for the better.

———

That June in 1989, I force myself to attend a banking event in Osprey, Florida, where a panel of three executives is slated to discuss loan commitment letters. The topic is nothing to light your hair on fire, and though he reads his speech from a yellow legal pad, one of the speakers manages to keep my attention, primarily because of his looks. He is tall, blond, and the most handsome guy I have seen, ever. I luck out and connect with him at the opening reception.

Looking at his name tag, I reach out my hand. "Hi, Steve. I'm Beth Owens. It's really nice to meet you," I say, hoping my anxiety doesn't show.

"It's nice to meet you too. I see you're with NCNB," he says, glancing at my red badge.

"Yes, I work downtown," I reply, stomach alight with butterflies.

"Do you work for Doug Mason?" he asks.

"He's our regional manager. Great guy."

"*I know him well,*" Steve replies. "*We used to live in the same neighbor-hood.*" He looks over his shoulder then back at me. "*Well, I better get over to my post on the panel. Good to meet you, Beth.*"

Well, I guess that's that.

I don't think much of the interaction until a week later when my room-mate, Julie, whom I met at the bank, asks if I want to go out with her and this guy she knows, Steve Knopik.

Steve Knopik? The terribly handsome speaker from the conference?

"*Oh, I don't know,*" *I say, trying to play it cool.* "*What's the setup—won't I be a third wheel?*"

"*With me and Steve? Nah, it's not like that. This guy Michael is opening a jazz bar in town, and I want to check him . . . I mean it out.*" *We laugh.* "*I didn't want to go alone, so I asked Steve if he was interested. So how about it?*" *I pretend to think about it a few more seconds before agreeing.*

When Steve comes to pick us up, the three of us pile into his company car. Shortly after arriving at the restaurant, Julie flits off to chat with the owner of the jazz bar, leaving Steve and me alone to get to know one another. I am a little intimidated by this man, so we sit there across from one another fiddling with our drinks and stumbling awkwardly from topic to topic.

It is rocky at first, but we both keep climbing. There is something charm-ing about the fact that he is a corporate big shot but also such a regular guy. And I can't explain it, but I have this feeling almost like I have known him in a past life. It's silly, I think, but still . . .

The cover band returns from break, and as the next jazz song starts up, Steve looks at the band then at me. "*Want to dance?*" *he ventures. A few songs later, Julie returns. When she sees Steve and me on the dance floor, she shoots me a wink. I smile and turn back to Steve. But what am I thinking, really? I mean, he is eight years older than me and a successful CFO—way out of my league. Even though I want to see him again, after we all say goodbye that night, I do not get my hopes up.*

But then Steve calls me at work to say hi. Then he calls again. "Let's have dinner," he says.

"I'll have lunch with you," I say. "On a workday."

A few days later, we meet at Bijou Café, a popular restaurant in an old, renovated gas station in downtown Sarasota. Wearing my favorite red suit, I walk in the front door to see Steve standing near the maître d' station. The maître d' grabs two menus and guides us through the main dining room, filled with men and women in business suits, to a table for two. We take seats across from one another other and place the white cloth napkins in our laps.

Unlike our first outing, the conversation flows easily. It turns out we have a similar affinity for wines and share some favorite wineries. I decide to up the ante and have dinner with him a few days later. Steve tells me that his mother, Ora Mae, died of cancer in 1985. The tightening around his eyes and the thin set of his mouth speak to how much he misses her. He tells me of his love for baseball and how he has been a St. Louis Cardinals fan since he was five years old. He talks of his former wife and shares some of the mistakes he had made.

Over successive dates, as I grow to see even more of Steve, our connection is undeniable. He starts to call me "Peach" after a line in one of his favorite movies, It's a Wonderful Life. *Behind his serene manner, I can see that Steve is also highly intelligent. He is always thinking, working on some plan or project. He can comprehend and analyze almost anything, and he never seems to beat himself up if one of his plans does not work out. Maybe I can learn something from him in that department, I think. And despite his success and his smarts, Steve is totally lacking in arrogance. His shyness I can handle. After all, I am quiet too. My universe begins to shift.*

——

Steve's voice pulls me out of my thoughts. He's laughing with our waiter. With Leanna in the hospital, I'd barely seen him smile in . . . what was it? Two weeks now. It was a welcome reprieve from the darkness that felt at moments like it was creeping in around us. I looked down at my menu, but the selections disappeared, and I was back in our courtship.

———

I am falling in love with Steve, and by contrast, my feelings for him finally make it clear to me that I do not love banking. Even though I work hard and enjoy my customers, the scrutiny of my overbearing boss takes its toll. Within days of my first nightmarish internal audit, the Crohn's disease I'd had since childhood flares up and nearly takes my life. An intense bout of abdominal pain and blood loss sends me to the ER where a colonoscopy diagnoses the problem: a ruptured artery in my intestine.

Over the next few weeks, I have two surgeries and spend nineteen days in the hospital. Steve is there twice a day, every day, stopping in on his way to and from work.

"Well," my mother says to me later, "I guess that answers any questions I had about Steve. Now I know how he truly feels about you."

The years roll by, and suddenly it is 1992. Steve and I do everything together, and it is clear there is nowhere else either of us wants to be. Yet while I entertain myself with the idea of marriage, in some ways, we seem no closer to making our union official. At one point, we travel to northern Italy together, exploring cathedrals and touring castles. Countless picture-perfect settings would have framed the ideal backdrop for Steve to turn to me with a little box in his hand. Yet a proposal never happens. It turns out that this man I am in love with is leery of marrying again. Is this as far as things are going to go for us?

The self-confidence I had fought so hard to build over the years begins to teeter. By the time Steve and I join friends at a Super Bowl party soon after our trip to Italy, I have started to lose faith in our relationship. Then, as I peer into the next room, I see Steve flirting with another woman. My heart begins to race, and I realize that after four years together, there are still parts of Steve that are out of reach.

That night, I lay it on the line. "Steve, we need to talk. Listen, I'm nearly thirty."

He holds my gaze, but he swallows hard. "Yes," he says, holding his breath.

"I want to be a wife, and I want to be a mother," I continue.

Steve shifts slightly, and he leans forward, giving me his full attention. Maybe this is not the best time for a talk, but I need to know if I am wasting my time.

"If we have no future together, then there's no sense in my staying in Florida anymore."

His expression shifts suddenly from that of a grade-school boy enduring a lecture from the principal to one of surprise. "What are you saying, exactly?" he says.

"I miss Virginia. I miss the crispness of the air in the fall. I miss snow. I miss being close to my family, Steve. And if you and I aren't going to start a life here, well . . . then I don't see why I should stay. I'm going back to Virginia. I'm going home."

Jaw clenched, Steve nods. He asks me not to make any rash decisions, and I agree.

Later that spring, with no grand romantic gesture, we decide to get married. Steve simply smiles one day over lunch and says, "Okay, Peach—let's do it. Let's get married." Yet what he lacks in pageantry and presentation, he seems to make up for in conviction. Steve is determined to prove he has learned from his past mistakes. He can make a second marriage work. He wants kids. There is no doubt in my mind that Steve will be an excellent provider and father, so with that, the decision is made.

———

Our courtship was dreamy in so many ways. I can remember looking over at him across dimly lit dinners and feeling like I was somehow implanted into the scene—this handsome, self-assured man I shared a meal with seemed almost unreal. Sometimes, I'd find myself startled when he looked at me; his eyes bore into my soul, and the shock of their truth—that he loved me—would stir me in a way that is hard to describe. But what warmed me most was watching him with our daughter. He was a father who made it clear that his children were the suns of his universe.

I remembered Steve giving Leanna her nightly baths as a toddler. He would come home from work, scoop her up, and cart her off to the tub in a bathroom just off of the kitchen. I would be cooking dinner while they splashed and sang these made-up songs, listening to this language that they shared, the ways that he delighted her, her squeals of laughter at his silly singing.

Now, Steve was being called to do the hardest thing he'd done so far—to stand steady for his family when the very ground beneath his feet was evaporating. Somehow, he seemed to be holding it all together, yet I knew better. In our own way, we were both losing it, getting stripped to the bone of our illusions that as long as we were good people and good parents, as long as we prayed together and cared for others, everything would be okay. We were adrift at sea, and there was no safe harbor. Even God didn't seem to notice us being caught in the riptide.

Sitting there at the restaurant, I was suddenly aware of Steve's voice. I looked up from the menu to find his tired eyes resting on me. "Peach, do you know what you want?"

Yes, I know what I want. I want our daughter to come home. I want the kids to go to Montreat and for us all to go back to South Africa. I want this nightmare to be over and for our family to be okay!

Instead, I nodded. "Yes," I said, "I'll just have a salad."

Chapter 7

"We're looking at a transplant. That's our only option."

We had entered week three of Leanna's hospitalization, and Steve and I sat dazed, listening to Dr. Andrews. At this point, we'd been drained of the vigor that hope helps to nourish.

"Leanna's heart is not responding as well as we had hoped. We suspect that the damage done to her heart is now beyond repair."

The words echoed through the cavern of my body. I was blindsided by the speed at which Leanna's plan of care was changing. It felt like being hurled in a boat careening horribly off course. Hope was now a distant acquaintance. Though we knew the doctors were doing everything they could, the possibility of death was becoming hard to escape. And heart donors have to die to give their hearts away. How could we pray for that to happen?

The doctors told us that hearts often become available in the middle of the night after a young person crashes a car. Our sleep became even more frayed as we prepared each night to be awoken by a dreadful, yet desperately needed, call that might never come.

While nights saw us tossing and turning, I was at least reassured that Leanna was in good hands. One nurse, Denise, was so attentive, almost like a mother. She moved quickly but carefully, documenting every little change as if Leanna were her own daughter. Eventually, Denise told us that she, too, had a sixteen-year-old daughter. Whenever Denise worked the night shift, I requested her.

Leanna now needed round-the-clock attention. At night, the lights were dimmed but never turned off. Machines beeped; alarms blared. I still hated the sounds, but Leanna's care team needed the continual updates the machines provided. They were necessary for her survival, and so I made my peace with them. Yet I wondered what Leanna could hear. Occasionally, we turned on the TV monitor in the room and played some of her favorite movies—"Finding Nemo" and "Despicable Me." We hoped that, through the fog of her sedation, they offered her some small sense of comfort, along with a respite from the sounds of the machines that surrounded her.

Even on the nights when I was reassured that Denise was watching over Leanna, as desperate as I was for deep sleep to restore me, it had become impossible. I was always exhausted, always close to tears, yet too wired to cry or to fall into any kind of release. I would lie down intent on a nap in our room at the Ronald McDonald House and then realize it was not going to happen. No matter how tired I was, my mind and heart were always with Leanna. Sleep would take me too far away from her.

I had lost my sense of self. Living day in, day out in velour sweat-suits, each emotion battered me like an avalanche. I tried to relieve the constant stress through more walks, deep breathing, and yoga here and there. I texted with Caryn, who over and over reminded me to take it one moment at a time and to remember the mantra, "faith and trust." I lost, regained, then lost again my precious sense of balance.

You can die in a hospital or have your life saved there, but any sense of normalcy I once felt in my day-to-day experience was gone. Every day, sometimes every hour, was like standing on the edge of a cliff. We were always on the verge of something—good or bad news about to come—and ceaseless anticipation depleted us.

In the tragic theater of the cardiovascular ICU, we saw infants born with weak hearts to parents who clutched each other and prayed. These little ones were touched by dozens of strange hands while their parents, who loved them most, wandered the corridors, unable to embrace their own children.

I was determined to keep it together by staying present and not allowing my mind to travel too far into the future. I shared little with others—nothing that approached the true depth of my fear. Steve suffered in silence. We were keeping it together. Getting through the days. We made sure Rogers was okay and that we were there for our daughter. We exercised and ate. But true feelings were stones that could shatter our glasshouse. While I sometimes longed for Steve to connect with me emotionally, I also knew that going there could destroy the delicate vessel we had created to contain our nightmare.

Sometimes, I would look at Steve and think, *No one else can feel what we are feeling.* Then I would remember all of the other families in the world who were losing medical battles. In our room at the first Ronald McDonald house two weeks before, I begged God not to take Leanna, but I knew the walls of that place had heard the pleas and prayers of so many other desperate parents. We were not alone.

Deep in the night, Steve and I sometimes woke to the sound of a helicopter approaching the hospital, its blades chopping the midnight air. Once, I saw Steve's eyelids flutter, then he rose from his pillow. Together, we listened for a moment. We heard the engines shut off after the helicopter touched down on the hospital roof. Another urgent case. Another desperate family.

In the midst of this, a few nurses on the floor thought it might be helpful for Steve and me to meet a mother whose son survived an infection much like Leanna's, seven years before. We met in the waiting room at the hospital. She was a soft-spoken woman in a simple blue dress. She offered me a smile and a hug before introducing her son, an unassuming young man in his mid-twenties wearing jeans and a t-shirt. His voice was faint and raspy, a result of the surgeries he'd had, including a heart transplant. During our time together he said little, but the tender glow of gratitude surrounded him like an aura.

As we sat and talked, the woman told me a story about the time she thought her son's life was almost over. "I went to the chapel here and prayed, 'Lord, help me to plan my son's funeral.'" And while she waited in silence, she suddenly heard a reply, calm and clear. "It's . . . not . . . time . . . yet."

Fascinated by her experience, I felt a flicker of curiosity. *Maybe I should try it*, I thought. After we exchanged numbers and said our good-byes, I walked into the tiny chapel with its modest altar and small stained-glass panel and took a chair. All alone in this humble place of prayer, I whispered, "God, please give me a sign." Yet while I desperately wanted some indication that God had not forgotten us and that Leanna, too, would be spared, my gut filled with fear at what the response would be. Or that there might not be any at all.

I listened and I waited. Yet as long moments passed, all I heard was a searing silence, the cruelest answer I could have received. Sitting still in that pained, deafening void, I felt alone. Abandoned. When I closed my eyes, deep swirls of red in varied shades swirled about.

What did it mean?

I opened my eyes.

I had come seeking comfort. I waited some more.

Nothing.

———

To keep the pumps running smoothly, the doctors put Leanna on blood thinners, which kept her blood from clotting. Yet the blood thinners caused her to bleed so much internally that sometimes blood bubbled out of the edges of her mouth.

Please, God, don't take her.

To relieve the excess blood and other fluid, the doctors inserted a drainage tube between Leanna's ribs, but it was only moderately helpful. So they inserted a second tube in her other side. They explained to us what they were doing and why, but all I heard was that my precious daughter had even more plastic tubes invading her body, causing more pain and discomfort.

I snatched my keys, turned on my heel, and headed down the hall.

"Beth, where are you going?" Steve called after me.

"I'm getting out of here!"

I made a beeline to the parking garage, planning to head to a nearby hotel where I had taken a few yoga classes, and jumped into my white SUV. I was about to break. *Maybe yoga will provide some calm—or anything at all to help me deal with what is happening,* I reason.

Alone in the parking garage of the hospital, I started the car and sat there. I couldn't bear to see Leanna suffer anymore. Boiling over with righteous anger, I began to scream.

"JUST TAKE HER!" I cried out then collapsed forward over the steering wheel, hot tears burning a trail of anguish down my cheeks. "FOR GOD'S SAKE, JUST TAKE HER!"

I don't know how long I'd been sitting there, but eventually, my tears dried. My breathing slowed. For several long moments, I sat back and stared out of the windshield at a concrete wall.

Then I found myself asking a question: "Are we doing this all for Leanna, or are we doing this for us?"

I held that question close like a tiny, delicate egg through the yoga class. As I drove back to the hospital, a resigned calm and clarity fell over me.

When I returned to Leanna's room, I took a seat next to her. It was just the two of us. I placed my hand on her arm and leaned forward. I took a deep breath.

"Leanna, sweetheart," I say softly, "you know we love you so much and more than anything, we want you home with us . . . but this is a decision between you and God. Whether you stay or go is not about me or what I want."

———

Perhaps God had already invited her to join Him. Perhaps God had explained my daughter's entire life to her before she was born, and this *knowing* gave her that unique ability that so many people noticed to live every day with love, laughter, and joy. Perhaps that was what made Leanna who she was.

One thing was certain. If Leanna knew that by leaving this world, her sacrifice would somehow help a lot of other people, she would have accepted God's offer and willingly surrendered.

Chapter 8

Many who cherished our girl came to the hospital and, day after day, filled the waiting room. Family, neighbors, school friends, people from our church. I did not ask them to come, yet I was glad they were there. I was relieved, too, that they asked nothing of us. We had nothing to give.

One morning, I was running back to our little room at the Ronald McDonald House to grab a jacket. As I crossed the footbridge that led from the hospital to our room and the parking garage, I was heedless of the bodies moving around me until I looked ahead and recognized a familiar face. "Wait, what? *Tracy?* When did you get here?"

"I flew in this morning," my sister said solemnly. "I couldn't stand being away. I needed to be here." Tracy, nearly three years older than me, had always searched for ways to reach out to others, whether it was with a fresh plate of cookies or a loaf of zucchini bread. Known to offer gentle support in an "under the radar" sort of way. I was quite surprised to see her standing before me.

Like the others who gathered in the waiting rooms, Tracy wanted only to be present—to serve as a visible reminder of the love that surrounded us. The doctors and nurses caring for Leanna were amazed by the outpouring of support. When Clay was back in Sarasota serving our church, he was always just a phone call away. In his absence, Tracy would often offer a prayer, spoken with an undeniable grace, which was essential. By now, my ability to reach out to God in any meaningful way was dwindling. While I still yearned for His help, the words lay outside my grasp.

I never dreamed that the mother I was—always so careful—obsessing over prenatal vitamins and exercise, insisting that Leanna make safe and smart choices, even all those times I'd wrangled with her just to brush her teeth or avoid candy, seemed so pointless now. My child, the daughter of disciplined and healthy parents, an athletic and cared-for child, was dying. My daughter, who just weeks before had a glow from the Florida sun, a constant grin, and the build of a rower, now lay there as helpless as anyone could be. All the logic in the world didn't resolve the way I'd pictured things with the way they were. My sister offered the words I couldn't say and didn't have. I was so grateful she was there.

My oldest sister, Faye, always thoughtful and organized, was willing to do anything that might be helpful as well. I wanted Leanna to hear familiar voices from people who loved her, so when Faye arrived from Maryland, I had her sit and read to Leanna the stack of cards she had received, the messages of which would usher clumsily from my own lips. I couldn't bear to read them. On the one hand, it was comforting and heartening to know of all the love out there for my daughter; on the other hand, imagining all this hope, all that ink, all that went into those letters landing on deaf ears, or doing no good, crushed me.

Steve's dad and his wife, Marcia, continued to come every evening. They would go through the ordeal of donning protective garb to sit with Leanna. Wally, wearing his teddy bear mask, leaned back on the little blue couch with his legs crossed awkwardly under the yellow paper gown. His long legs and lean body recalled Steve, and even in Leanna, I could see some of his traits. Here he was, two generations older, while my child, who'd not yet lived long enough to attend her own graduation, atrophied in her bed among a mass of cords and ever-watchful machines.

Caryn continued to reassure me. "God is always with you." She referred to God as Spirit, and her own connection to divinity was vast and deep. "There's so much we don't understand, Beth," she told me, sensing my own confusion. "That's why we have to rely on faith and trust to get us through."

One day, I received a text from James Amato, who had been my hairdresser since before I was even married. *Remember to take care of yourself, Beth*, he wrote, then added, *If you want, I am happy to drive up and give you a cut and color.*

It was a kindness I was happy to accept.

Friends from church, the Schwabs, gave us four bracelets with a silver angel wing and a leather cord as a token of their love. I leaned over Leanna's bedrail and wrapped hers around her puffy fingers. One more symbol of the love and prayers that showered her.

With the outpouring of support, Steve and I received lots of well-meaning gestures, and we were grateful. But sometimes, even the simplest questions, like "What can we bring you to eat?" were too much to process. We tried to take it in, but the reality was that we were in raw survival mode, hanging on to one moment at a time. While we tried to open ourselves to the love around us, we had a sense that for some people, their gestures were more about meeting their own need to be supportive. And that's okay, but as much as possible, we tried not to let ourselves feel pressured to care for others by defining ways they could care for us.

———

Amid all this attention, I tried to create space for Rogers to visit his sister. He also continued to spend time at Florida Studio Theatre where he could immerse himself in other roles and other stories—ones less frightening than the drama that had taken over his family. But there was no way of pretending that things were getting better.

At some point during that third week, Dr. Simon declared, "Leanna is the sickest person in the hospital." It was a stunning declaration. A gut-punch when we were already reeling. We kept such details from Rogers, yet the seriousness of his sister's struggle was painfully clear.

One day, Rogers and I were on I-75, driving from the theatre to the hospital. Cars whizzed by us and while indie music played in the background, I asked Rogers about his day. Then I saw it. Coming up the on-ramp just to our right was a white hearse. I had been constantly looking for signs, and if this was a message from God, it was one I did *not* want to receive.

Rogers noticed a shift in my demeanor and turned to where I had glanced then back again. I'm not sure if he saw the hearse or not. The mood in the car became suddenly somber. Rogers asked, "Is Leanna going to be alright?"

More than anything in the world, I wanted to say, "Yes, of course."

Instead, I blurted. "I don't know."

Rogers turned and looked out the side window.

As we drove to the hospital, silence fell over the car.

———

Day in and day out, what I hated most was not being able to really touch or connect with my daughter. But whenever I spoke to her, I had to believe she heard me, even when she gave no sign. In those moments, it felt as if her soul was floating outside her body, hovering over us all. She looked like an angel despite all she had been through.

When a group of women in the prayer shawl ministry of our church learned about Leanna's illness, they crocheted a shawl for her. The card read: *May you be cradled in hope, kept in joy, graced with peace, and wrapped in love.* We draped the rich teal fabric over Leanna. Looking at her covered from head to toe in their woven wishes, I remembered my baby girl as a toddler clinging to her knitted security blanket, dragging it everywhere she went.

As Leanna's spirit seemed to come and go, once in a great while, I would see her blink and surface from the sedation. In those moments, Leanna's eyes would grow wide as she looked around, filled with anxiety. Paralyzed by the medications, I couldn't imagine what it was like for her to wake up and realize that she could only move her eyes and her tongue.

I didn't know how to mother her then, but I would rush to her side.

"Your heart is sick, Leanna," I told her. "We're trying to fix it." I was afraid of saying too much. I didn't want her to worry, but I didn't want her to be confused, either.

During a wakeful moment, I once asked her, "Leanna, if you love me, could you stick out your tongue?" knowing this simple gesture was something she could likely manage.

Through the tubes, I saw the tip of her tongue appear. My girl was in there, communicating the only way she could. I turned away to wipe a tear, my heart in complete shambles.

———

Every Sunday throughout Leanna's time at the hospital, Steve and I ventured to a local Catholic church that was an easy walk from the hospital, so close it was visible from Leanna's room. Steve had grown up Catholic, and I was just grateful for a sanctuary.

As Leanna entered her fourth and final week at the hospital, the priest delivered a sermon that felt like a message for us. It was based on a story found in the Book of Mark about miracles produced by Jesus, including one in which he healed a twelve-year-old girl.

Jesus crosses a lake by boat and when he reaches the shore, a crowd gathers around him. A man named Jairus, the leader of his synagogue, falls at Jesus's feet and pleads with him, "My little daughter is dying. Please come heal her."

The priest described the scene as Jesus accompanies Jarius to his house, followed by the murmuring crowd. Among those who have gathered is a woman who has suffered from a bleeding disorder for the last twelve years. As the group presses in close to surround Jesus, the woman, who is behind Him, reaches out and touches His cloak. Just like that, her bleeding stops. Instantly, Jesus is aware that a miracle has taken place. He turns and asks, "Who touched me?" The woman confesses it was she, and Jesus speaks to her to comfort her.

Jesus then continues to follow Jarius to his house, but on the way, someone comes to Jarius and tells him that his daughter has died. Jesus walks into the house, along with a few of his disciples and the girl's mother and father. The girl's body is already prepared for burial. Jesus approaches the girl and says, "My child, get up!" Suddenly, she rises.

I had heard versions of the sermon before and knew the point was to remind us of the divinity of Jesus. Yet as I sat there and listened to the priest, I wondered, *Am I the bleeding woman? If I push forward, if I have enough faith and believe fully, will our daughter be healed?*

We knew the sermon could be just a coincidence, but we couldn't help but take it as an indication that Leanna would be healed. Sitting there in the sanctuary, I prayed with more focus than I had in days.

Dear God, please grant me wisdom. I hunger to trust you completely.

And again, I waited. Everywhere I turned I searched for signs and looked for rainbows.

There in the hospital, so many of us were trying to trust God. Day after day, we gathered in the waiting rooms and prayed, yet the confines of that building often felt more like a prison than a place of resurrection. Would we receive *our* miracle?

Chapter 9

After much waiting, wishing, and praying, we finally got our rainbow. Steve, Rogers, and I were out for a casual dinner on the waterfront when it appeared.

"It was pretty funny," Rogers was saying, telling us about his day, "one of the kids just—"

Rogers stopped mid-sentence as he looked off in the distance, over my shoulder. Steve and I turned and traced his line of sight. There in the slowly declining summer sun, just beyond the bobbing mast tips of a cluster of sailboats, a rainbow stretched down through the clouds to brush the water somewhere in the distance. We looked at one another and dared to share a smile.

Back at the room at the Ronald McDonald House, Rogers pulled out his laptop and flipped it open. "Mom? Dad? I've got to show you this video." He sat cross-legged on the floor. Steve and I knelt on either side of him, looking down at his screen. Rogers hit a few keys; then, as piano music started to play, he placed the laptop on the bed so Steve and I could get a better view.

The opening shot was a close-up of Chris Martin lying on an old mattress. I glanced down and read the title of the video: "Coldplay—The Scientist."

As the lyrics floated from the computer, here and there phrases became stuck in my mind.

How lovely you are.

Let's go back to the start.

Then Martin's body rose in a jerking motion from the mattress. A kid on a bike rode backward behind him. The story was running in reverse, taking us back to some earlier point.

Nobody said it would be this hard.

Martin walked backward down a street, past a park, and through a railroad yard, all the while, singing the song forward.

Such a shame for us to part.

Finally, he made his way through the woods to the prone figure of a young woman, lying on the ground, unconscious, next to a car with its windshield missing. He climbed into the car, then the body of the girl rose off the ground and rested in the passenger seat as shards of glass levitated and fell back into place, reconstructing the window. The car began to roll backward up a hill, through a broken fence, and back onto the road, where it had swerved to avoid a truck that had crossed into its lane.

As the video ended, Rogers closed the laptop, and once again, we sat in silence.

If only.

The thought threaded us together like a spider's web. At that moment, we three were bound by our longing for a different outcome. A chance for a do-over. If only we could go back to the start and change something, anything, to make things different.

———

The next morning at 6:45 a.m., Steve and I walked our usual path to Leanna's room to meet with Denise, the night nurse, before her shift ended. When we entered the room, we were met instead by Dr. Everett.

"You're here early," I said; I hadn't expected her cardiologist to be at the scene so early in the day.

I felt my body stiffen.

"Yes," he replied, "I wanted to check Leanna's vitals and while I'm here, check her out completely. Her little toe is blue, which, along with other indicators, shows that her blood is not circulating properly."

I felt Steve's arm circle my shoulders.

"I'm concerned that a blood clot has settled in the apex of Leanna's heart," the doctor continued. "We will schedule a TEE—a transesophageal echocardiogram—to give us a view of the back of her heart. The blood thinners we have administered are not breaking up the clot."

I wandered to a chair beside Leanna's bed and sat.

"When will you perform the procedure?" Steve asked.

"We are trying to get it scheduled now."

What next? I wondered as I peered over the bed rail at my daughter. I heard Steve sigh and glanced up to find him standing there looking at me, and our wordless exchange spoke volumes.

In a huff, Steve turned and left the room for his morning run, then he stopped and poked his head back in. "I'll see you back here around nine for rounds," he said.

I nodded. "I'm right behind you. I've got to get out of here too."

I made my way to the parking garage, then crossed town toward the boardwalk in search of an outdoor yoga class. It was early on a weekday, and the area was subdued with only a few people strolling or rollerblading. I looked around, but no one was practicing yoga.

As I wandered, I saw a group of six middle-aged women in t-shirts, shorts, and leotards lying on towels in the shade of a large oak tree.

"I this an exercise class?" I asked as I approached them.

"No," one grinned, "just our lame attempt to get some exercise together. Would you like to join us?"

I stood there looking at the small sea of smiling faces and from nowhere, tears began to fall. "My daughter's in the hospital, and she has a serious heart condition," I blurted. "I'm afraid. I'm so afraid she might not make it."

They sat up.

"Oh, honey," one woman said.

"We'll pray for you," another chimed in.

"Let's pray right now!" one declared.

In a flash, the women were on their feet. Like a compassionate army, they rose as one and formed a circle. We clasped hands and bowed our heads.

"Dear God, we ask for your grace," one began. Suddenly it was if we had been friends for a lifetime. I was a perfect stranger, consumed with despair, yet as I stumbled in my grief and confusion, without question or hesitation, they caught me. As we stood there together, I felt the energy of their presence and their love work its quiet magic.

"Amen."

"Amen," we all repeated. Then, one by one, each of them hugged me.

I wiped at my eyes. "Thank you. Thank you so much. I better get back to the hospital," I said then turned to walk on.

"Wait!" one of the women cried as she held out her hand signaling me to stop. "Don't go anywhere. I've got something for you." She turned and sprinted across the lawn to her car parked on the street. A minute later she reappeared with something in her hand, which she held out toward me. It was a book of devotionals, wrapped in cellophane. Later, I wondered where the book had come from. Was it something she had bought for a friend and decided to give to me instead? Had some angel tapped her on the shoulder and told her to purchase it even though she wasn't sure why? I held the book of faith in my hands and, somehow, didn't feel as desperate. Maybe God *was* still around.

Yet later that day, we learned that the results from the echocardiogram were not good. As Steve and I sat listening to the details of the procedure, there was only one fact we cared about—Leanna's heart was not recovering. It underscored the reality that a transplant was our only hope.

Leanna needed a new heart, and she needed it immediately.

———

Through all the various prayers, advice, and recommendations, one that floated to the surface in our haze was the name of a priest in town who was known for being a miracle healer. Consumed with worry and waiting for word of a new heart, Steve and I decided to accept his help.

He was a slight man, about sixty-five years old. Born in South America, he had dark hair and olive skin. When he arrived at Leanna's room, he wore a black robe with a colorful stole. As he floated in, he barely looked at Steve or me but instead fixed his eyes on Leanna. Even with her eyes closed, she looked radiant.

The priest focused on Leanna with such intensity, it was as if Steve and I were no longer there. He mumbled a prayer of healing. Steve and I leaned in, straining to hear the divine invocation that was being made on our daughter's behalf. "Lord, you are the one and only almighty healer. We ask for your blessings upon Leanna, for she is your beloved child." The priest then dipped the tip of his right thumb into a vial of olive oil scented with balsam. With a light touch, he drew the sign of the cross on Leanna's forehead while speaking softly. "Leanna Knopik, I anoint you with oil in the name of the Father, and of the Son, and of the Holy Spirit." Then he closed his eyes and prayed silently for another minute or two. When he opened his eyes, he took a deep breath and without looking at us, left the room.

That was it.

I'd expected to be comforted by the priest's ritual on Leanna's behalf, but all I felt was the cold glare of devastation. How desperately ill was our daughter, and how desperate had we, her parents, become?

———

The faithful mother we had met the week before whose son had received a heart transplant came back to the hospital to visit Leanna the next day, a tattered copy of the Bible in her hand. She stood by Leanna's bedside and read aloud a long passage. It was probably about faith or healing. Truth be told, it was a blur to me—part of the storm of prayers and blessings that swirled around us from visitors, through cards and gifts, and on CaringBridge.

We were now nearly four weeks into this miserable journey, Steve and I struggling to find a way through all of it. Perhaps some new drug, an angel heart donor, or a medical breakthrough would suddenly appear.

But none did.

In a rare moment alone, as I sat cross-legged on our bed in the Ronald McDonald House, head in my hand, I asked aloud, "Why is this happening?"

Since Leanna had become sick, my prayers were divorced from any sense of serenity. I no longer expected peace or rapture. The most I hoped for was some sort of clarity. But the effortless space of faith and trust that allows for clarity was inaccessible to me. I was panicked. Everything—the doctor's words, the incessant machines, even the well-wishes—felt blaring and jumbled. I was entangled in emotions, none of them divine.

It's over. Leanna isn't going to make it, my frantic mind told me.

Still, in my heart, I could not give up hope that somewhere, from a place beyond human understanding, a miracle might find its way to us.

That there was some way to save her, and we were going to find it, or it would find us.

I didn't know it at the time, but while I struggled with hope in those final days, Steve had a talk over lunch with his friend, Greg, the cardiac surgeon.

"Steve," Greg told him as delicately as possible, "at this point, Leanna is being supported entirely by machines. This can't go on forever. You may need to make a tough decision soon."

Steve absorbed Greg's words, then opted not to share them at the time—to protect me from further anguish. But in some way, part of me already knew.

Chapter 10

On July 17, twenty-eight days after Leanna was admitted to the hospital, the surgical team set out to perform a third open-heart surgery to install yet another device. The intra-aortic heart pump, we were told, was often to support patients until a transplant was available—coined, "a bridge to transplant." Leanna's situation was now even direr because she had been taken off of the transplant list while she recovered from a urinary tract infection.

Hours into the procedure, Dr. Simon stepped out of the OR to have a word with Steve and me. "We have some . . . some very surprising news," He paused and stood there in his surgical scrubs with a puzzled look, his icy-blue eyes staring back at us. "When we disconnected the ECMO, Leanna's heart started to beat on its own. I'll be honest," he said, "we're not quite sure what to make of it."

My breathing became rapid. Our daughter's brave battered heart was battling on.

"Can you believe it?" Steve said. "Our girl is so strong. She's a fighter." His voice held an excitement I hadn't heard from him in weeks.

"So instead of installing the new device," Dr. Simon said, "we've decided to observe Leanna for a while to see what happens."

Just forget all these machines! I thought. *Maybe she doesn't even need them!* It was as if someone had poked a hole in the dark cloud hovering above us, and a ray of light illuminated the mountain of my frustration.

As Steve and I stood in the threshold of Leanna's door, scrub-clad medical staff wandered around stunned and dazed. Others leaned back in rolling office chairs at the nurses' station, staring at the ceiling. It was a scene from either a disaster or a miracle. We had to believe this was a positive sign.

Once again, I felt an imaginary bar descending and snapping in place across my lap, pressing me down into my seat.

Here we go . . . Hold on!

After two hours of watching and waiting, the OR team decided to reconnect the ECMO and see how Leanna fared. Perhaps her heart could recover after all.

Yet during the procedure, Leanna's body began to bleed uncontrollably.

When Dr. Everett emerged from the surgical suite to give us an update, he looked nearly lifeless himself. His face washed of all color for the first time since we met him, his expression was devoid of any trace of optimism. "Leanna is *very* sick," he told us emphatically. "Her bleeding is out of control, and we are packing her chest to try to stop it." He took a deep breath. "Once she is stable, we will continue to monitor her for a while, so it will be some time before she's back in her room."

Steve and I closed our eyes and lowered our heads in disbelief. "Oh, my gosh," I said. A surge of nausea flooded me. Feeling weak in my knees, I turned to join our faithful family members, to embark on yet another stint of waiting.

Hours later, a nurse came to find us. "They're bringing Leanna back to her room now."

Steve stayed to speak to the nurse while I plodded down the hall to Leanna's room to await her return. Within minutes, an entourage of medical staff shuffled through the doorway, maneuvering Leanna's bed, along with the army of machines that supported her. They took a few minutes to arrange the equipment and check the various readouts, then everyone except the nurse who was monitoring the ECMO filed back out. Leanna's body had been through hell, but that fine thread of life she held onto had gotten her to this moment. My daughter was alive. She was fighting. She was giving literally all she had and for what? I thought of all the people praying for her. I needed her to know that what she was going through meant something.

Even with the nurse present, it felt as if Leanna and I were alone. I leaned over her bed and rested my hand on hers.

"Leanna, there is something very important I need to say, and I need to say it now. You are making a big sacrifice for all of us, for everyone." I struggled to keep my voice steady as I watched her lay there, motionless. "Your beautiful soul has decided to take this path for the growth of others. *Thousands* of people are now praying for you through Caring-Bridge, some of whom have never prayed before. You are leading people to God." I paused. "Yes, Leanna, *you* are leading others to God!"

It was my only comfort—this image and feeling I had in my body that Leanna was like a great magnet, pulling people together, creating a collective movement of souls toward faith.

But at what price?

Motion in the doorway prompted me to look up. Steve was standing there, his face drawn.

"Now that she's stable, Beth, let's get out of here," he said.

"Yeah," I nodded. I turned back to Leanna and whispered, "I love you, sweetheart."

We made our way to the parking garage then hopped in Steve's white sedan and drove toward the boardwalk.

Our wellspring of emotion had run dry, and there was nothing to say. Steve flipped on the radio and after a few minutes, a string of familiar notes grabbed my attention.

"This sounds like Keane," I said, glancing at the lighted screen on the dashboard. "Oh, wow. I was right!" I exclaimed. "They must have a new album."

The song was "Silenced by the Night." Obsessed with this British rock band, Leanna, Rogers, and I knew every word to every song on their first album, *Hopes and Fears.* I leaned back in my seat, closed my eyes, and let the simple, soulful sound and haunting vocals fill the space around me.

As I listened and allowed my mind to dream, it seemed that the lyrics had been written just for Leanna and me. The rich melody and the words felt hopeful, and my heart started to soften as we continued driving. Or maybe it was just my *attempt* to find hope in such a dire situation. All I knew is that something in me was beginning to *shift.*

Tom Chaplin sang about being silenced by the darkness—separated from the light but rising together, wanting things to be as they were before . . .

We see less at night, but we hear more. Background sounds grow more powerful when all else is quiet.

How do I rise from here? I had found myself wondering as Steve first pulled the car out of the hospital parking garage. *How do we rise and find our best selves, no matter what's happening here on Earth?* As if to answer, there was this song telling me, offering me a new way to connect with Leanna beyond the obvious and ordinary, linking us soul to soul.

As human beings, the path of knowing is so narrow. In a universe trillions of miles high and just as wide across, what we see is limited. Yet when we allow ourselves to open, entirely new ideas and experiences become available to us. As we sped on from the hospital to the boardwalk, I felt myself moving to a higher place. *Leanna and I will find our own way to rise,* I thought. I saw the two of us riding in my car with the windows down, music blaring, and our hair whipping in the wind.

I was lifted and brokenhearted all at once. Leanna's illness had silenced her, and as a result, pieces of me were being forced to seek new ways to connect. I felt myself, for the first time, venturing into the gap between what we know in this place and what lies beyond it.

———

After dinner with Steve and a terribly emotional day, I slipped into Leanna's room, took out my phone, and held it next to her ear. "Leanna, listen," I whispered. "It's a new song from Keane. I think you're going to love it." I pressed play and the melody wound around us. Even if all that held Leanna there was a fine thread of hope, for those moments, she *was* still there. And I could share the joyful agony of that sacred space with her.

Chapter 11

"I think Leanna has had a seizure, Mrs. Knopik," Carrie declared with tears in her eyes. It was Wednesday, July 18, and one of our favorite nurses had found me in the hallway.

"How do you know?" I asked.

"Her eyes opened wide then shut several times." Her voice trembled as she spoke. "The doctor will be here to talk with you in a few minutes." I pressed onward to Leanna's room, praying Carrie had somehow gotten this all wrong.

I took a seat next to Leanna's bed and noticed a gaping feeling of emptiness as the machines droned on. *I wonder if she's even in there.*

Dr. Everett soon appeared outside of Leanna's room with Steve trailing behind.

"Beth, come out here for a minute," Steve said, motioning me to the hallway. "You've heard the latest, I take it?"

"Yes, I just spoke with Carrie. I pray to God she's wrong."

"Within the hour, Leanna will be taken down for a CAT scan, and we'll know for sure," Dr. Everett offered.

"Okay, I've got to walk around. My head is spinning. I'll be somewhere on this floor if you need me," I said.

It's odd that dire tragedies can take on a dark, dull rhythm, but that's what had happened during Leanna's hospital stay. There were the daily reports from medical personnel, the long, defeated walks down the gleaming, yet dreary corridors of that building, and the blue vinyl chairs that became like extensions of our bodies. It's hard to think of how nightmarish situations can become a new way of life, but they do; then, there are moments that jolt you out of the rote depression and into something primal and wrought with dread. That encounter with Carrie, the suspicion of my daughter's seizure, it all felt like we were speeding toward a cliff, and I was jolted into profound fear. It was this fear that engulfed me as I paced the hallways, unable to relax or find any sort of stillness.

All I *really* wanted was to be with Leanna, as hard as it was. It felt like our time was running out, so I headed back to her room.

I was met by the searing sight of Dr. Simon slumped in a chair just outside of Leanna's room, with a green surgical cap on his head, which he was shaking slowly back and forth. I approached him.

"Dr. Simon?"

He looked up at me, pained, and shook his head again. His blue eyes were red. "I'm sorry," he whispered. "I'm just so sorry."

Sorry? What was he saying to me? First Dr. Everett, then Carrie, now Dr. Simon. One by one, the health care providers who had stood so tall and confident were wilting before our eyes. If they did not believe in Leanna, if they had lost faith in her ability to recover, what chance did she have?

I felt my teeth clench. "You can't give up on her," I scolded. This man was our ticket to wellness—to Leanna getting better—and he was telling me he was *sorry*?

"It's not over!" I half-shouted and stormed back to the waiting room where I threw myself into the chair. Steve stared at me for a moment but didn't speak, and I didn't divulge my newfound fear, nor Dr. Simon's apparent defeat. I was too furious for words.

Finally, a nurse summoned us, and with heavy steps, we made our way back to Leanna's room to wait again.

Time bent like a modernist painting. Somewhere between twenty minutes and three hours later, another nurse entered the room to announce that the results of the exam were in. She motioned us to follow her to the neurologist's office.

"Thank you. We know where it is," Steve said, rising. Steve took my hand as we shuffled through the common area, past the nurses' station, to the doorway of a tiny office. A man with short, gray hair and wearing a white coat was sitting there looking at a computer screen.

"Hi, I'm Dr. Daniel, the neurologist," he said, rising to shake our hands. "Please, take a seat."

We perched, backs rigid, on a pair of angular metal chairs facing the desk.

"I have reviewed Leanna's CAT scan and confirmed that she has blood on her brain. You can see it here and here," he said pointing to dark spots on the screen. Dr. Daniel's expression was flat. I sought reassurance in a softened gaze or an encouraging smile, but there was none to be found. The doctor continued, and I struggled to focus on his words, to stay with him when all I wanted to do was run screaming or collapse in a heap. Anything other than just sitting there and accepting whatever he was about to say. "Normally, we would do brain surgery but . . ." he paused then continued. "With Leanna's body in the state it's in, I'm afraid . . . well, she could never survive that."

For the second time in our lives, Steve and I sat there across from a man in a white coat giving us news that was impossible to fathom. Once again, we were stunned into silence.

My eyes drifted beyond Dr. Daniel to the plain white wall behind him, where I saw our lives showing like a movie.

———

Leanna, Steve, Rogers, and I are celebrating Leanna's sixteenth birthday. We're in Colorado, skiing during the kids' spring break. After a spe-

cial dinner at the base of the mountain, joined by our friend and ski-pro, John, we bundle up and trudge out in our snow boots to the slopes to set off a few fireworks and light wish lanterns. The starry sky is awash in sparks of color.

"Happy birthday!" we shout. As Leanna looks up with each explosion, her wide smile is illumined by the light. Then, I watch Rogers pull out two thin square packets from beneath his ski jacket and hand one to me.

"Let's light this one first!" he declares and kneels in the snow. He opens the packet and begins to unfold its contents. Rogers had come up with the idea of releasing the lanterns into the Rocky Mountain sky on Leanna's birthday. He stands and holds up the delicate structure of sheer paper attached to a metal loop. Steve jumps in to help. Rogers pulls out a lighter and touches the flame to a small square at the bottom of the lantern. As Rogers balances himself on the angled terrain, trying not to slip, he holds the base steady, and the lantern begins to expand into a glowing oblong. "Okay, here we go!" he shouts and releases the lantern, which quickly thunks to the ground then begins to tumble down the slope. "Ack!" Rogers exclaims then gives chase, scampering off down the hill. Steve grins and shakes his head as Leanna and I erupt in laughter.

Finally, we succeed in launching the lanterns. As they drift off into the night, I make a silent wish—every mother's wish for her child—that the year ahead brings my daughter great joy.

We turn and walk back to our condo, and as we pass through the parking lot, we see an old, rusted-out yellow Pinto. I leap in front of it and throw up my arms. "Surprise! Here's the car we promised you for your birthday!" I yell. "Stand in front of it. I'll take your picture."

Leanna rolls her eyes and shakes her head. "Mo-om!"

It is such an exhilarating moment, one that swells my heart with pride and joy and love almost too large to carry. I find myself wanting my girl to be reminded of the enormity of our love for her.

Later, before Steve and I turn in, I pull out my phone and send Leanna a private message on Facebook. "Happy happy birthday, my lovely Leanna. Sweet angel . . . Love, Mom and Dad."

——

Suddenly, there was a snap. The big black wheel of the projector began to spin fast, the ribbon of film beating as it slapped against the machine. I was back in the office with Dr. Daniel looking at me. I felt my whole body begin to fall as if the floor and all the ground beneath it had opened up to devour me.

Trancelike, I shifted in my chair and looked at Steve, my rock, hoping to see his jaw set in a resolute proclamation that we would fight on. But I could not see his face because he was folded in half, his head buried in his hands.

Then it's true, I thought. *It's over.*

Myocarditis and its countless side effects were going to take her.

I breathed in a long, deep, slow breath, and the air held me upright while inside, I collapsed like a rag doll.

In the last few days, I had stopped asking for miracles. Instead, I asked God for clarity.

Please light the way. Help me see what is right and what is best.

It was my one prayer that was answered.

It was time to take Leanna off the machines. Time to tell our family and loyal friends that we had lost the fight.

It was also time to bring Rogers home from the church retreat.

We called Clay.

——

A few days prior, when it seemed like Leanna may be improving, Rogers had left with Clay for the middle-school Montreat youth conference in South Carolina.

On Wednesday evening that week, as he sat listening to the keynote, holding hands with his girlfriend, Elizabeth, one of the conference staff walked up to his row, leaned in, and whispered to Rogers. "Please, I need you to come to the lobby."

Rogers initially thought that perhaps he and Elizabeth were in trouble for holding hands. *Is that not allowed?* he wondered. Then as he entered the lobby, he saw a familiar figure standing there and his heart fell. It was Clay, and his expression told Rogers everything.

"Your parents called. They want you home."

Clay and Rogers hastily packed up and drove all night to reach the hospital just after sunrise. Clay was mostly alone with his thoughts as Rogers, stretched out in the back seat, drifted in and out of sleep.

Clay delivered Rogers to the Ronald McDonald House and as Rogers walked toward us, bag slung over his shoulder, I could see in his eyes that he knew. Steve and I opened our arms to pull him close. We found a seat in the common area. "Rogers, listen," Steve whispered, "we have to let your sister go." Our grips on one another tightened.

"This may be the hardest thing we ever do," I said, hearing the words as if someone else was speaking them. I was in shock, and I felt like all I could do was pull lines out of a box of things you say in times when words fail. It was the only way I could get through. The only way I could be strong for my son. "We are going to get through this together, okay? All of us together." I felt Rogers nod, his head pressed into my shoulder.

No, not all of us, I thought. *We will never be all of us again. Not without Leanna.*

Rogers's eyes were droopy. "How about if you get a little rest, first? Then we'll . . .," but I didn't finish the sentence.

I tucked him into a makeshift bed we'd prepared for him on the floor. Eventually, he dropped into sleep while Steve and I tried to rest beside him, waiting. This day would be the hardest day of our lives.

———

A few hours later, it was time. We roused Rogers to set off on this last visit to Leanna, a terrible prospect no young sibling should ever have to endure.

"I've been texting Christina and Josh, and they both want to say goodbye. I told them I would call them so they could talk to Leanna. Is that okay?" Rogers asked.

Christina had been away at summer school, and Josh was with his family in the Adirondacks. Neither of them dreamed Leanna would not be there to greet them when they returned.

Rogers's ever-present thoughtfulness prompted tears as I nodded: "Of course."

The three of us rose and filed out of our tiny refuge for our last walk to Leanna's room. We moved slowly, holding hands, finally climbing onto the elevator where Steve pressed number five. "Going up!" the cheerful child's voice announced through the speakers.

The elevator seemed to struggle upward, burdened by the weight of our devastation.

Finally, we entered Leanna's room, where my beautiful darling rested in her bed. One of the strange ironies of Leanna's condition, or one of her treatments—I don't know which—was that her skin had the bronzed look of someone who'd been at the beach all month. Her puffy hands and the broken capillaries on her nose were the only indicators, beyond the medical equipment, that she was not simply napping.

Rogers's slender frame slid between two machines as he took his place by his sister's left side. Steve stood at the foot of her bed, and I was to her right. We could not hold her, so this was the best we could do to surround her with our love.

Rogers pulled out his phone. "Christina? Yeah. Here she is." He held the phone up to Leanna's ear. None of us knew what Christina said or if Leanna heard it. I've always been told that hearing is the last to go, so I tell myself, even to this day, that she did hear the words of her best friend, the words of the girl who'd first detected something was wrong. Rogers repeated the process with Josh, both calls just a brief minute. Steve and I looked on, proud of our strong and thoughtful son, our hearts ripped open as we closed a precious part of our lives.

Phone set aside, it was Rogers's turn to say goodbye. He was trying to be brave. To hold it together. But the big sister who had always been so lively, so engaged with him, was propped up in bed, motionless and draped in the prayer shawl with her eyes shut, never to open them again. He leaned over, his face close to hers, and began to cry. His tears escalated and through sobs, he mustered one thank you after another for the everyday things she did to shine her light in his life. "And thank you for all the times you took me to Sunny Bunni," he sniffed. His tears became a deluge as he choked out his final words to Leanna. "I'm going to miss you so much."

Rogers straightened and we turned to Steve. His face was bound in a grimace. He was so taut, so tensely wrapped that I waited for him to crack into a million pieces. But somehow, Steve pressed forward. Still, he was so wrought with emotion that he was only able to utter one word. "Goodbye," he choked.

It was my turn. I had no idea how to muster the courage or the words to speak. Maybe my hope of "Silenced by the Night" and the image of Leanna and me riding carefree in my car still lingered, telling me it was *not* the last time. With a grace born in the moment, I reached down and took my daughter's hand.

"Leanna, I'm not going to say goodbye because I *know* you will always be with me."

I paused and gave her a long look. My baby girl. The one who taught me how to be a mother, who was now leaving far too soon. I had no idea who I would be without her.

And yet my final words rang true; I felt in every molecule of my heart a love for her so big and so unyielding, I couldn't imagine a world in which the two of us would truly be separated.

Then, Dr. Everett entered the room, along with a few of the other doctors and nurses. They paused and took in the scene as Steve, Rogers, and I stood shocked and frozen around Leanna's bed. The team looked distraught. Their best efforts had fallen short. Their confidence in their ability to heal Leanna was not a self-fulfilling prophecy. They, too, were shaken.

Finally, Steve and I looked at one another. Then he turned to Rogers, holding out a hand. Rogers walked into his father's embrace, and the two turned to leave, Steve's arm wrapped around his son.

We had made the excruciating decision not to be with Leanna for her final moments of life. It was what Greg thought was best. "Spend time with her and then step out," he said. "If you want, if it would help, I will be there with Leanna and her medical team."

The moment had come. We were on the precipice. Greg stood in the doorway awaiting his cue to enter. I took one last look at Leanna, covered shoulders to toes in the prayer shawl, then turned and followed Steve and Rogers. Greg slipped wordlessly into the room, and at that moment, I realized he was right—whatever was to happen, I could not watch Leanna go.

Clay entered. He, too, would shepherd Leanna through her last moments here.

There is a phenomenon, they say, wherein tragic accidents appear to unfold in slow-motion, as humans approach their fate. Steve, Rogers, and I drifted into the waiting room, each gesture slow and pronounced, suspended in time even as we collapsed into our chairs to wait. A throng of close family members moved in and surrounded us.

A short time later, Greg appeared in the waiting room and took a seat. Looking down at the floor, he said in a voice barely louder than a whisper, "She's asleep."

Strangely, I felt relief. No more suffering for our sweet girl.

———

Later, Clay told us that Leanna left us without a struggle. That she felt no pain as she departed on her blanket of light.

As they were turning off the machines, Clay began to sing the old spiritual "Swing Low, Sweet Chariot." If she was still present, he wanted the last words she heard to be comforting, and this was a song he and Leanna had sung together in church.

I have heard Clay say before that crossing over from life to death may be frightening for those left behind, but those departing are not alone. All their tears and fears and pain are gone, and they are in full communion with God and with perfect love. I have to trust that was true for Leanna as she released her last breath.

PART
TWO

Chapter 12

I t was over. Just like that, everything shifted. In the weeks prior, hours felt like days, even years. Then, in a matter of minutes, Leanna was gone.

It can't *ever* be that the death of a young person happens without some bigger purpose. That's clear to me now. Yet, in the days after Leanna's passing, nothing was clear. Nothing made sense. All our prayers, everyone on CaringBridge, the Coldplay concert, and all the energy and faith directed toward Leanna's healing had fallen short. The God I'd relied on all my life was nowhere to be found.

I gave up on God the day Leanna died. In doing so, I had no idea what I would find or how I would survive. But over time, what spanned the canyon of my grief was something far greater than the faith I had known. Even on the day of her passing, the signs were already there, whether I saw them or not.

Back in the summer of 2012, our friend Doreen heard about Leanna's illness. She and her husband joined the tribe of supporters following Leanna's plight on CaringBridge. In 2020, eight years after Leanna's death—nearly to the day—on an otherwise ordinary afternoon, an email from Doreen appeared in my mailbox. I read the typical greeting, and then my heart skipped as the message took an unexpected turn. She wrote, "There is one memory that involves you that I've neglected to share before now. It remains one of my most profound life experiences. I regret that I've waited this long. I am not sure why. Perhaps I was waiting for inspiration, to get it 'perfect' in order to do it justice." Eventually, Doreen realized by waiting to tell us, she was withholding something of value, so she finally decided to share the following experience from the day Leanna died.

———

It's early afternoon on July 19, 2012, and Doreen is driving home on Florida's I-275 South, returning from a quick trip to Ocala. As she reaches St. Petersburg, she notices All Children's Hospital in the distance, which brings Leanna and our family to mind.

At that moment, a song Doreen has never heard before starts playing on the radio. "If I die young, bury me in satin," the young female sings, and the lyrics penetrate Doreen's consciousness. Doreen is certain beyond all doubt that Leanna has passed. Tears begin to flow.

Then, Doreen glances back at the hospital and sees something that leads her to slow down—an enormous double rainbow that appears as if it is coming right out of the hospital. Doreen looks around to find no evidence of rain; the pavement as far as she can see is bone dry.

Now awash in tears, Doreen pulls to the side of the road. Staring at the incredible sight before her, she listens as the song on the radio continues. "Lord, make me a rainbow, I'll shine down on my mother; She'll know I'm safe with you when she stands under my colors."

Doreen cries as she has never cried before, and she says it is for us, but also for so much more. At that moment, she is convinced that God is ushering Leanna into His kingdom in full glory. It is proof to her that we are never alone, and the promise of everlasting life is real.

"And I have never looked at a rainbow the same way again," she wrote.

———

It's hard to describe how I felt when I received Doreen's message. Deeply moved. Inspired. Filled with awe, gratitude, and, most of all, love. Yet not surprised. Because in the years since Leanna's passing, I have seen so much evidence of her presence and felt the deep knowing of my daughter's connection to something so much greater.

When I think back to how I got to where I am today, I can recall those early days when our loss was so fresh and raw. Not all of the details are clear, obscured as they are by the veil of sadness that descended over me. I was barely making it from one minute to the next. All I could do was keep moving. Performing menial tasks transported me through the day. But in some ways, even this was hard because with each dish I washed, each shirt I folded, I was moving farther away from the last time I saw Leanna. It's a tug and pull, a yin and yang, a sadness together with a sense of accomplishment. On the road of grief, most milestones aren't visible in the distance or even as you pass them. It's only looking back that those seminal memories and moments blend into a story of healing.

The day Leanna died was an ending in the physical sense. A bright light had gone from this world. My daughter was gone. That fateful day, after Steve, Rogers, and I left Leanna's side to join our devoted family and friends clustered in the waiting room, all I could think about was how I wouldn't see her beautiful face or feel her arms around me anymore.

Yet there were the arms of others around me. Rogers. Steve. Brothers and sisters, parents, and other loved ones. One pair nearly identical to the next. The hugs were welcome and needed, and while I was aware of them, I was unable to receive the comfort they meant to provide. Something inside me had gone adrift, and even the most tender hug could not moor me.

———

As I sat there in the hospital waiting room, slumped in my chair absorbing Greg's words, I became aware that Steve was looking at me. His mouth was moving. I squinted at him through my fog, orienting toward the sound of his voice.

"We're finished here," he said, his tone flat with finality. "Let's go home."

Weary and dazed, I stood and reached for Rogers, who was wiping tears from his face. Taking Steve's hand on one side, with the other I guided Rogers toward me. This was it. We were leaving. We were crossing the chasm.

As the three of us turned toward the elevators, our support network gathered in Leanna's room to carefully pack up her things. The gifts, cards, signs, the t-shirt she had made for work camp, the small bottle of holy water, and Lucky, the stuffed German shepherd Josh had tasked to watch over her. Steve's younger sister Valerie, along with Chris, also agreed to post an update to CaringBridge. After everything I had shared with the thousands of kind hearts who were trudging along this path with us, this was one thing I could not bring myself to write.

Later, Tracy told me that Leanna, or rather her body, was still in the room when our small crew shouldered their labor of love. "Beth, she looked so peaceful," Tracy said, her eyes glistening. "All of the machines were gone, the room was quiet, and it was just Leanna there in the bed. She looked so small and just—" Tracy covered her mouth for a moment as she steadied herself. "She looked at peace."

Steve leaned forward and pressed number two on the elevator panel. Through the haze, I heard the sing-song youthful voice. "Going down." The cheer of it seemed to mock my pain.

We descended then slowed, the elevator giving a last little lurch as it came to a halt. The doors slid open, and we drifted over the threshold and down the hall for the last time. Step by excruciating step, we crossed the footbridge toward the parking garage, passing doctors, nurses, and parents escorting their children who had just been discharged and were going home. Their glee, knowing the worst was behind them, only magnified my loss.

Later, when I thought about that walk, I had no idea how my body carried me over that bridge. No clue as to why I did not collapse to my knees. No explanation for how I was able to leave my daughter's body behind. Yet I did. We did. The three of us.

Maybe it was shock.

As we entered our room at the Ronald McDonald House and began to gather our things, if the building had caught fire at that moment, I might not have noticed; or worse, I might not have cared.

I followed Steve and Rogers to the door then paused and glanced back at the empty room. Sometime after we departed, the staff would clean and ready it for the next family. Part of me wanted to offer a prayer that their outcome would be different from ours, but I was empty of words.

As our loaded car emerged from the dark hollow of the garage, I glanced at the clock. It was 1:33 p.m., and there wasn't a cloud in the sky. I squinted into the sun, just as I did on that glorious day we had brought Leanna home as a newborn. With our precious baby secured in the back seat, our lives together had just begun. The road before us seemed to hold nothing but promise.

Now, as we rolled down the interstate in silence, our son in the back-seat staring out the window, the sun illuminated a different world. One that was exquisite but fragile, like the shiny soap bubbles we used to blow for the kids in the backyard. The bubbles would catch the sun with their smooth surface and display for us a glistening rainbow, then *poof*, in the next moment disappear.

That's how life is, I thought. Bubbles burst. Prayers go unanswered.

When people die in a hospital, they are surrounded by a small circle of devoted doctors and nurses. Family is present. CaringBridge had grown that circle for Leanna, but in the wider world, there was no recognition that anything had happened. I looked out the car window at people busy with their day, oblivious. How could they just walk down the street, go to work at some faceless office building, or drive at a time like this? Couldn't they see what had changed? Didn't they know what we all had lost?

I wanted to roll down the window and scream, "What's wrong with all of you?"

Feeling betrayed by strangers, I reached in my pocket and retrieved my phone. I needed to connect with people who knew me and knew what today was.

Leanna is now with God, I texted.

The replies came quickly.

Totally unfair, read one.

I felt her release, read another.

That is beautiful. I know He has her already.

Finally, we turned into our driveway then sat there for long moments as the garage door slowly raised. Inside, we climbed out as a gleaming white Honda Civic stared us down, asking where Leanna was.

Bag by bag, we unloaded the car, and the rituals that followed felt dull and meaningless. Separating laundry into piles of darks and whites to protect the whites from the dye of other garments. We could save these clothes but not our daughter. Putting toiletries back in their place. We could bring these items home but not our daughter. Stacking cards on the kitchen counter. We could read these messages of hope but never again hear the hopeful voice of our sweet Leanna.

We're bringing so much home but not our daughter.

At some point, I looked up to find Steve standing before me, car keys in hand. "I'm going to get Desi and Lucie."

The dogs! The breeder had boarded them all this time. When Steve announced that he was going to retrieve them, I was reminded of yet another longing, only this one *could* be fulfilled. "Oh, thank goodness!" I exclaimed.

As I thought of Desi with his classic Doberman coloring of black with brown markings and Lucie with her dark brown body with splashes of tan, I missed them with an intense ache. I needed to care for them. To walk them. To feed them. To soak in their wordless understanding and unconditional love. And to relish in their total obsession with the present moment, which was all I could handle.

Rogers had gone upstairs to his room to message with friends. As I watched the door shut behind Steve, I found myself wanting to call out to him. The aloneness that descended was sudden and jarring, and before I knew it, I felt myself start to sink, as if someone had opened a drain and I was about to be sucked in.

Keep moving, a voice inside me commanded. Grateful for this simple guidance I rushed to the laundry room and began loading the washer. I knew if I stopped, I might fall into a pit too deep to climb out of.

Now in foreign territory, I stood there in my own home, unable to contemplate what was next. Every moment was vacant—an empty, terrifying void. The future had been stolen from us.

When we left the hospital Steve said, "I want to get as far away as possible from this place and everything about it. I want to be home." And I did too. But looking around and feeling the lack of Leanna's presence all around me, I realized home wasn't the same anymore.

In fact, nothing would be the same anymore. The life I knew just thirty days before was over.

After Steve returned with the dogs, we agreed with Steve's dad and sister to assemble the family for dinner. Somehow, we prepared a meal—baked chicken, roasted potatoes, green beans.

With the dogs at our feet, eight of us ate. My heart raced. I looked out the kitchen window toward the pool, where I saw eight-year-old Leanna floating on a pink innertube, her feet dangling in the water. She smiled at me and waved. "Hi, Mom!"

"Mom?" I turned and saw Rogers looking at me. "Is it okay if I invite a few of Leanna's friends to spend the night tomorrow night?"

"Yes, of course. I think that's a good idea."

I looked down at my plate. This living hell might just swallow up the rest of my life. Would I ever find peace? Was it even possible?

How does a parent grieve their child?

After dinner, Caryn arrived with her daughter. When I texted her earlier to confirm Leanna's passing, she asked if I would like her to come by. I said yes, knowing Caryn only wanted to offer quiet support and would ask nothing of me. For an hour or so, Caryn and her daughter Katya, a lovely young woman of eighteen, simply sat with me on the sofa, saying virtually nothing. But it was what I needed. Consolation was a task that words could not accomplish. While their quiet and unassuming presence could not diminish my pain, I was not alone.

By the time Caryn left, Steve was already in bed. For as long as I'd known him, he was nearly always asleep by 9:00 p.m. and up before dawn. Rogers found comfort in the rec room watching a movie. Unlike his father, he was a night owl and often turned in after us.

Somewhere across town, Leanna's crew teammates, including the seven girls in her boat, along with the coaches and some of the rowers' parents, had arranged to meet at the private beach on Sarasota Bay where the crew practiced. One of the crew picked up a stick and drew a huge heart in the sand and wrote Leanna's name in the middle. Then, those who gathered traced her name with fresh flowers. As the sun touched the horizon, the girls in Leanna's boat walked their empty hull into the water, then offered their flowers and tears to the bay.

I looked out over our empty house, darkening as the summer sun bid its goodnight. In those first hours at home, the love of family surrounded me and held me together, but how was I going to get through the rest of my life?

Over and over, my thoughts played the same refrain. *She's gone, and nothing will bring her back.*

As I navigated the rawest, cruelest punishment there is, I began to wonder about the people who had prayed for Leanna. Would they become atheists? And after all of this, what did I believe? I had no clue.

That first night home, I pulled back the covers on my bed.

Before climbing in, though, I felt drawn to a warm shower. Perhaps it could soothe my weary soul. In the bathroom, I turned the knob to start the flow of water. As I undressed in front of the mirror, I gazed at a woman completely lost in her despair.

If this is a nightmare, please wake me up!

Then I caught myself again. Who was I pleading to? Myself? God? *God is clearly absent.*

I stood there in the steamy shower, the gentle water raining down on my shoulders. Alone with my thoughts, I sobbed. I cried not only for the death of my daughter but for the cruel betrayal of the *one* who led me to this place.

Finally, I mustered myself from the shower, dried off, and dressed for bed. Afraid of the night, afraid to be alone in this brutal, dark time, I reached for the bottle of Xanax my doctor had called in for me. *Better make it half a pill to be safe*, I thought, worrying about the possibility of becoming addicted. I stared at the two pieces sitting there in my palm, "Forget that idea," I thought, then popped them both in my mouth.

I climbed into bed next to Steve and fell quickly into the bottomless black of dreamless sleep. Two hours later, my eyes snapped open. Within seconds my mind turned to Leanna and full-blown panic set in.

She's gone. She's really gone! God, no!

Electrified by this dreadful realization, I bolted out of bed, padded to the kitchen, and planted myself on a stool. I cradled my head in my hands, unable to believe the hand we'd been dealt. Tears welled.

I glanced at the clock. Not even midnight. Would I sleep at all or just spend the night haunting the halls?

Finally, I made my way back to the bedroom where I noticed something odd. The light in the linen closet next to the bathroom was on. It was an automatic light, so that could happen if the door wasn't fully closed, yet when I saw it, I couldn't help but wonder . . .

Leanna? Is that you?

No, that's crazy.

But . . . the door is closed. The light shouldn't be on.

Beth, it's a glitch. Just call the handyman tomorrow and have it fixed.

I walked over to the door and gave it a firm nudge. Sure enough, the light went off.

See? It just wasn't closed the whole way.

I turned toward the bed, where within moments, I was back to sleep.

When my eyes opened next, I glanced at my watch. 3:00 a.m. Suddenly, I realized what I was seeing. Once again, the closet light was beaming across the bedroom, lighting up the opposite wall.

Leanna, is that you? If it is, can you find another way to show me? You're frightening me.

I rose once again and jiggled the door until the light went off. *For goodness sake!*

Was she playing a game with me?

After catching my breath, I settled into bed a third time and, once again, managed to succumb to sleep.

Chapter 13

Whena I woke for the third time, a muted light filtered through the window. The sky was a dark shade of turquoise that, to my tear-filled eyes, took on a menacing hue. The wall across from the linen closet was dark. An eerie stillness pervaded the house.

I stared out the window, my body dead weight, then I glanced over to Steve's side of the bed, but he wasn't there. *Probably out for a run*, I thought.

The dogs started to stir the moment they sensed my wakefulness. I took a long breath, freed myself from the covers, and managed to lift my head from the pillow. I sat up and swung my legs around until my feet touched the floor. I lingered. Using my hands to push off the bed, I stood, feeling the weight of my body on the hardwood floors. Like a puppet on a string, my feet and legs started to propel me forward as I made my way to the bathroom sink. Most mornings, a splash of cool water helped get me going. Not this morning.

Get moving. Get moving, then keep moving. This voice in my head was mine but distant—as if a part of me better able to cope had taken charge.

Aware of the whines coming from the next room, I lifted one leg, then the other, sliding gym shorts up to my waist. I managed to pull a t-shirt over my head. In old rubber flip-flops pierced with Lucie's teeth marks, I scuffed across the house to the utility room and opened the door to the garage. Desi and Lucie charged past me into the yard in search of squirrels. Surrounded by dense trees, the sun's rays were just starting to peek through. I watched the dogs for a moment as they picked up new scents. Standing there in the driveway, feeling the weight of the tropical dampness that is Florida in July, I wondered how I would make it to nightfall.

Just take the next step, the voice said again.

Weet-weet-weet! The high-pitched chirping of cardinals called me to search for them. They were perched in a tree across the street.

HOOO! HOOO! Two owls called out in the distance.

I closed my eyes and felt nature reaching out to me. I wanted to reach back, to feel the embrace of something bigger than me. Could I find Leanna out here among the birds and the trees? Was it her voice speaking to me through these bird calls? Or was it just a mother's desperation?

I wandered further along our gravel driveway. The old oak trees were draped in scarves of Spanish moss, giving them the look of wise old sages from some other world. I bent to pick up the Sarasota *Herald-Tribune*, its plastic bag dripping with dew. I pulled out the paper to glance at the headlines. In a few days, Leanna's obituary would be printed. But that day, the newspaper spoke of distant things—the real estate market and a presidential visit to the state.

A bark called my attention, and I watched as the dogs darted across the yard. A year or so before, I had been out walking them, contemplating my life. Where I had been, where I was going, and what it was all for.

Now, instead of answers, I had even more questions.

Where am I going? How did this happen? And why? As a rower, Leanna had excelled at one of the most physically demanding sports there is. How could she have died of an infected heart? There was no sense to be found.

Newspaper in hand, I called the dogs and trudged inside. Robotically, I dropped dried food and diced chicken into their bowls and refilled their water dishes.

Keep moving. Just keep moving.

The saying goes that the journey of a thousand miles begins with a single step. The distance that stretched before me felt endless. And yet that's how it began—with one step. Then it continued with another, then another. Each was unremarkable at the time, yet collectively, they transported me through the minutes and then the hours.

——

Several years after Leanna's passing, during his sophomore year at Loyola Marymount, Rogers created a short audio piece for his sound mixing class. Rogers being Rogers, he waited until the last few hours to pull it together, yet the finished product was remarkable. Even he wondered what he might have accomplished had he taken more time with it. The piece was a rhythmic spoken-word poem about Leanna during her final days, her final hours, and beyond. My heart reeled with pain as I listened to Rogers tell of driving all night with Clay, then arriving at the hospital, knowing what we were about to tell him. He recalled how Steve and I embraced him and whispered in his ear, "Rogers, listen—we have to let your sister go," and reassuring him that somehow, we would get through it together. After saying goodbye to Leanna, he recalled those final steps from her room and his inability to imagine life without his best friend, feeling "lost," he said, "with no direction to go but forward." Footsteps sound in the background, signaling our long trek down the cold, sterile hallway. Rogers says as we walked away, he recalled the lyrics to a Chris Brown song Leanna had played for him a few years before. In the song, which begins to play over Rogers's voice in the background, Brown asks how life will go on from here, then answers—eventually, we will run again, but first, we will crawl.

When I heard the audio piece, I wondered yet again: Was some part of Leanna aware of what was to be? Was she unconsciously preparing her brother for a day her soul knew was coming?

That day and for many days after, I crawled, almost literally, dragging my body, heavy with grief, from moment to moment, wondering, *Will I someday get past this ceaseless anxiety?*

———

It was impossible to believe that I would ever feel peace again. And while it took time, early on, I was blessed with a few brief moments when I glimpsed the impossible, and they gave me the gift of planting a seed.

The night Leanna passed, Valerie—an experienced yoga teacher—asked if I would be interested in a private session, explaining that some gentle yoga might be helpful. "Okay," I said, "sure." I had no idea if I would be able to make it through the session, but at least I wouldn't have to leave home, and Valerie would understand if I had to stop or take a break.

After feeding the dogs that first morning, I unrolled an orange yoga mat onto my bedroom floor. Valerie joined me, laying out her mat. "Beth, I'm going to take you through a series of restoration poses. We'll begin by sitting comfortably."

I watched as Valerie sat with her legs crossed and her eyes closed.

I imitated her.

"Let's focus now on some deep breathing. Breathe in . . . filling up your lungs . . . and now exhale . . . letting it all out. Breathe in deeply, breathe out . . ."

I knew this part of the yoga session was critical—that to reduce my anxiety, I needed to inhale fully and exhale completely. Shallow breathing only amplified the chaos in my soul.

With humility and skill, despite her own broken heart, Valerie led me through pose after pose designed to calm my racing thoughts and exhausted nervous system. I followed her instructions for nearly an hour as she guided me through the proper form for each pose.

She's gone, and she's never coming back. She's gone, and she's never coming back. She's . . .

As I fell deeper into my breath and into my body, the tape that played over and over in my mind began to slow.

"Beth," Valerie said, her voice whisper-soft, "let's settle you on the mat now for *savasana*." I lay on my back, feeling the spongy material against my skin, a thin cushion atop the hardwood floor.

"Now place the soles of your feet together and allow your knees to fall to the sides." Valerie propped a pillow under each knee then slid a smaller pillow under my head. "Feel the ground beneath you, supporting you."

Valerie pulled out her iPhone and placed a pair of headphones over my ears. "Ommmmmm . . ." a voice sounded once, then again. Valerie slipped out of the room, and I fell into the sacred sound, releasing my full weight onto the mat.

"Ommmmm . . ." I had no awareness of the source of the chanting, whether male or female. I was drawn instead into the reverberation, as if their vocal cords were merely an instrument through which a greater voice was sounding. The vibration filled me, traveling through every cell of my body, and transported me to a place of weightlessness. For a few God-given moments, my rampant negative thoughts were silenced, replaced by a simple awareness of the gift and comfort of that sound. I let the chant hold me, suspended, in a place without a name, beyond thought. The cloud of grief still lingered, but as I lay there, surrendering to the rare calm of transcendent breath, my nervous system fully exhaled into a state of peace.

Then, with a jolt, my eyes popped open. Just like that, I was flooded with anxiety.

Please, no, not yet. Let me be here a little longer!

But it was too late; I was submerged so deep I had lost all sense of what direction was up. Or where I might find the light.

Yet those few blissful moments gave me an awareness I clung to—an answer to my desperate yearning for peace again. I now *knew* that even if I have to practice yoga every day for the rest of my life, this was an access point to peace. Though it had lasted only precious seconds, that brief interval was everything. I had bobbed to the surface and broken through. I had gasped fresh air. Something in me was oriented to rise, and when it was time, when I somehow loosened the shackles of grief, my heart would know what to do.

———

I made my way through the morning fixating on routine tasks. Buying myself time, I relied on the most mundane chores to carry me to a time when the present moment wouldn't feel so fraught with danger. The undertow was always there, threatening to drown me, and I knew that struggling against the truth would only make it worse. Staying busy was my way of floating, of letting the current take me farther into shore while I caught my breath.

Steve, too, did his best to keep moving, cleaning out the refrigerator, going to the grocery store, and checking in with his assistant at work. He had kept a hand in his job duties over the last month, checking emails periodically, and, when necessary, signing paperwork his assistant brought to the hospital. Though Steve had been fully present the whole month, and though we were both still exhausted and overwhelmed, I could tell that part of him was starting to transition back into work mode. I couldn't blame him; it was something to focus on.

Rogers spent most of the first day watching movies. That morning, we decided that Leanna's service would be on Tuesday. Rogers then took it upon himself to write about his sister's service on CaringBridge, asking everyone to wear bright colors to celebrate Leanna's memory. Between movies and posting, he also texted and Skyped with friends. Both his friends and Leanna's were pulling together, and I was grateful they had each other to lean into.

By lunchtime, I was running out of regular chores in the kitchen, so I moved to my office where I began to organize and clean out desk drawers. As I reached for a stack of papers on my desktop, I froze. There on a small pad of paper was Leanna's writing. "Hi Mom!" the note read. My heart skipped. I stood staring at Leanna's loving handiwork. She had traced the words over and over in black ink as if she'd wanted to be sure I would see them.

—

Steve and I decided to host a gathering that evening. Family had already begun arriving in town from Virginia, North Carolina, and Missouri. While the thought of being around so many people was daunting, we also needed them. Grief is a magnet that can alternately pull and repel. Like Rogers and his friends, the lot of us were drawn together, bound to one another by our loss. There was nowhere else to be but with each other.

Just before 6:00 p.m., a dear friend and former neighbor arrived with a huge assortment of Asian food. As I looked at the spread arranged on my kitchen counter, I realized she must have spent all day cooking, using every serving dish and crockpot she owned. It was more than enough to feed all thirty people we were expecting.

One of the great benefits of these gatherings was the copious amounts of food—always more than we could possibly eat. As people finished, my sister Faye organized the leftovers into smaller servings that she put in the freezer. These easy meals would sustain us over many days. The food was a quiet blessing and another opportunity for me to learn to receive.

I left tears on many shoulders that night. An hour or so into the evening, I glanced across the room at Steve, who was pouring himself another glass of wine. His eyes were dry, the numbing effects of alcohol providing a buffer between himself and loss.

By 9:00 p.m., the gathering was still going strong, but anxiety began to flood my nervous system again as I anticipated the long night ahead. For once, I wasn't worried about being a good hostess. I asked a friend to encourage folks to wrap it up and honor our need for sleep. The house emptied quickly.

"We love you."

"We're here for you."

"I'm only a call or text away."

As the last guests departed, I realized I needed desperately the love they were taking with them. Their lives seemed so much more manageable, their sorrows portable, whereas mine was made of concrete, an immovable weight.

Several friends of Rogers and Leanna stayed behind to spend the night with Rogers. Adrift on their own small ships of loss, they rafted up into a tightly-bound group.

That night a huge storm broke. "Mom!" Rogers called from the back porch. "Come see!"

I joined the kids, clustered around a candle-lit coffee table by the pool. In the velvet sky, there was a crackle, then the sky lit up with a crash of light.

"Mom," Rogers said, turning to me, "it's Leanna. We just know it."

I looked beyond him into the darkness.

Bang!

Another burst of light illuminated the night.

Chapter 14

On Saturday, two days after Leanna's death, we began preparing to cross the last threshold of immediate grief—the funeral.

That morning, Valerie led another "grief yoga" session, this time including Steve. Once again, yoga created crucial space for me to connect with the present moment and to tame the chatter that cluttered my thoughts.

Afterward, as I stood in the kitchen scanning leftovers for lunch, there was a knock at the door. A moment later, Steve appeared, followed by Clay, who was clutching a Bible and notepad against his chest.

Steve and I gathered around the kitchen table with Clay as he flipped through his notepad, pen in hand. We bowed for a quick prayer.

"Okay," Clay started. "I've laid out a framework—"

Steve rose from his seat and began to pace. "We want this to be a celebration of Leanna's life," he said. "That's the most important thing."

Clay nodded. "Yes," he said, "I understand. We want to honor Leanna, and to remember her in love and joy. At the same time . . ." he paused and shifted slightly in his seat. "At the same time, a Christian funeral has certain . . . protocols. There are guidelines."

"No," Steve scowled. "In the last four weeks, we've had more than our share of protocols. We're not doing that. We're not making Leanna's service full of doom and gloom."

"I understand," Clay repeated, "but . . ."

He continued talking, but his voice blurred in my mind.

Steve shook his head. As an executive for many years, he was used to making decisions—with others deferring to those decisions. But in matters of church etiquette, Clay outranked him. Tensions mounted as the two batted their visions for the service back and forth.

Finally, Clay said the word "protocol" one too many times.

"We want this to be *upbeat!*" Steve erupted.

Here we were, fighting for Leanna's service to be more about harmony and joy. Over the next few moments, the irony seemed to sink in with Clay and Steve, too, and we took a collective breath.

"Okay, I hear you," Clay nodded. "Let's try this another way."

Eventually, we worked it out; there were enough elements of church protocol to satisfy Clay's obligations as an associate pastor, yet the overall tone would be in line with Leanna's personality, honoring her spirit.

That night, we hosted yet another gathering for those who had arrived that day. More hugs, more condolences, more tears.

———

So automatic was our Sunday morning routine that, having finally returned home, the programming kicked back in. After a light breakfast, Steve, Rogers, and I began the day preparing for church. Visiting family came along to support us, and together, we took up the entire back row.

It wasn't until the service began that I started to question my presence there. I looked around at the faithful parishioners in the large sanctuary, and suddenly, I felt different from all of them. They seemed so

Steve nodded again and I looked at him for a long moment. I had no idea how we were going to host a guacamole competition days after Leanna's funeral. But then again, I didn't know much of anything anymore. And if Steve felt like it would help him, I could go along with it. Maybe it would help Rogers too. For their sakes, I was willing to give it a shot.

"Okay," I said, "I want to support you, but I can't make any promises that this will be good for me."

In the end, like so many hours in those first days and weeks, the scene of eight couples scattered around our kitchen chopping, stirring, and tasting was too surreal for me to process. I did my best to mix in, but in the end, when everyone had had enough to drink to lose track of me, I disappeared into my bedroom and closed the door.

———

Hosting parties. Working tirelessly. Keeping a mental log of the St. Louis Cardinals' wins and losses that season. Steve did his best to soldier through the wreckage of our lives in those first few weeks. How he acted as if life was somewhat normal troubled me.

He thought his job was to be strong and help everyone else get through this, especially Rogers and me. As a result, he didn't spend enough time on himself and his feelings. I also sensed that for Steve, if it wasn't time, it wasn't time. Hopefully, at some point, he would get there—to the place where he felt like he could really start processing what had happened. I prayed for Steve, but I didn't push him. It was all I could do to handle my grief and be mindful of Rogers; I didn't have the strength to try to manage Steve's process as well. To cope in the day-to-day, Steve tried to fill some of the void with beer and wine. That time of drinking and vacancy was hard to watch, but I had to let it play itself out. I knew he was coping the best way he knew how.

attentive, heads turned toward the pastor, eagerly awaiting the word of God. Just like I used to do.

What am I doing here?

For so many years, God had been like a best friend to me. As the organ played, I was transported back to another church, at another time.

———

In the sixth grade, I leave our neighborhood Methodist church to attend a Baptist church where some of my friends have gone. I want to try it out, so Faye drives me there every Sunday, drops me off, and picks me up. Over the next few months, every week, I go to Sunday school and morning worship. During some of the services, I watch intently as adults and kids like me are baptized. Unlike other churches I'd gone to where the pastor would take holy water and draw the sign of the cross on someone's forehead or sprinkle it on their head, Baptists go to greater lengths. At the front of the church sits a baptismal pool, built right into the wall behind the pulpit.

I look on as those about to be baptized don special white robes, descend into the water-filled chamber, and move next to the pastor. Each person crosses their arms in front of their chest. Then the pastor supports their back with his left hand and holds a handkerchief with his right over their mouth and nose as he slowly leans them back into the water, briefly immersing them. When they come out of the water, they are purified—in union with Christ.

I watch in awe. How I want that for myself. My heart is ready. God is calling me.

Finally, my day comes. On Palm Sunday evening, when I am eleven years old, I get to wear my own white robe. The choir sings from beyond and above the pulpit, their voices rejoicing.

I've waited all day with nervous excitement. Finally, when it's my turn, I walk into the chamber then pause to look out at the several hundred parishioners in the church's vast sanctuary. With my glasses off, the crowd is a blur.

Slowly, I descend a few steps into the temperate, waist-deep water, walking toward the pastor. I give him my handkerchief.

"Beth Ann Owens," he says, "you are a beloved child of God. I baptize you in the name of the Father, the Son, and the Holy Spirit." His left hand supports my upper back, his right hand gently covers my nose and mouth. He dunks me backward, fully in the water, quickly raises me back up, helps me up out of my River Jordan, and walks me to the far set of stairs. My blonde hair is soaked, my robe dragging behind me.

At the top of the steps, a staff person meets me and leads me back to a dressing room where I change into dry clothes. Only then do I realize that, with my robe wet, you can see the tiny pink flowers on my underwear. My brief flash of embarrassment dissipates quickly. Instead, I am awash in love in its purest form; I am closer to God than I have ever been.

———

Now, with the sun streaming through the stained-glass windows, I looked around at the backs of my fellow congregants—many of whom were like family, yet I felt confused, vacant, and alone.

Chapter 15

"Mom, Dad, I have an idea," Rogers announced between big bites of cereal Monday morning. "You know those stretchy bracelets people wear in memory of someone?"

"Yes, of course," I replied.

"I want to have some made in Leanna's honor. I'll sell them for five dollars each and give all the money to the hospital. They'll say, 'Team Leanna.' I'll order green ones since that was her favorite color. What do you think?" he asked, waiting for our reaction.

I looked at my son and words failed me. While Steve and I were awash in sorrow, he was already thinking of a way forward. Already taking up the mantle of generosity and service.

I reached across the counter and squeezed Rogers's hand. "I love it, Rog. I think that's beautiful."

Through this action, Rogers prompted me to think about how we might remember Leanna at our home. How we could keep her memory alive. Now, when I talk to people who have lost loved ones, especially children, I gently urge them to create a project or devise a special way to remember them. When you lose someone you love, especially a child, you will do *anything* to keep their memory alive. The idea that you may someday forget them, that your memories will fade, is a horror too difficult to contemplate. Today, Leanna's memory is kept alive in many ways, but it all began with this loving act from her brother, which ended up raising more than $1,000 for the hospital.

———

Finally, it was Tuesday, the day of Leanna's service. On one hand, it felt like if we could just get to it and through it, perhaps something would shift. On the other, it was a day I hoped would never come. The finality it brought was a truth I still could not accept.

It was a busy morning as we hustled to get ourselves and the house ready for the day. I had asked James to come and style my hair. I needed to look my best.

He arrived right on time. Hairdressers and their clients share a bond like a mix of friendship and therapy. For years, I'd shared countless stories with him while I was sitting in his chair, basking in the care he was giving me. I'd divulged so many ideas, dreams, emotions from whatever life might have been throwing at me each of those visits.

There was so much I wanted to say to him, but meaningful words fizzled into mundane chatter of an ordinary day.

"Hi," I said. "Please, come in."

"Thank you," he whispered.

With teary eyes, James and I held a long embrace as if to absorb each other's pain.

"I'm just so sorry," he said in the gentle voice Leanna had known since before she was born. Taking a deep breath, I led him to my bathroom where I had everything laid out—brushes, combs, hairdryer.

James stood behind me and swept a comb through my hair as we stared at each other in the vanity mirror. I took a steadying breath. "I don't know how I'm going to get through today."

James stopped combing. I again looked at him, and he gazed back at me. He didn't say a word, but his soft, unflinching presence created a container for my grief. Once again, just like Caryn and Katya sitting with me on the couch the night Leanna died, not filling the void with words was best. Letting my pain be normal, letting all my feelings be okay in some way grounded me.

When James pronounced me ready, I stood and looked at myself in the mirror wearing a coral dress. The contrast between my perfectly styled hair and tired, sunken face startled me. Though I see myself every day in the mirror, this haunted woman was a stranger.

I walked out to the living room where Steve and Rogers were waiting.

"The car is here," Steve announced as he folded his eulogy and tucked it in the pocket of his blazer. None of us could believe we were leaving to attend the funeral of our beloved Leanna, but one thing we knew for sure—we had each other.

We arrived to find Clay waiting in front of the church, and he escorted us through a side door and down the hall to the parlor. Finally, at the appointed time, 10:30 a.m., we walked single-file into the narthex. There on the communion table in front of the sanctuary was an enormous flower arrangement in the shape and colors of a rainbow. Next to the table, a poster-size black-and-white framed portrait of Leanna perched on an easel. In a burst, I felt my heart expand, love rushing in to fill the emptiness, gratitude embracing grief. There she was, right there. Posed in a black turtleneck sweater against a black background, her blonde hair bright, her smiling face glowing. It was as if she was floating right there before us. I'd seen the portrait before, of course, but this felt like the first time it ever appeared before me. And this person in the frame was the most beautiful woman I'd ever seen.

I directed a quick glance toward a sea of mourners in the sanctuary. People were packed shoulder-to-shoulder, with even more standing behind the pews and spilling out into the narthex. Love was Leanna's legacy, and I wasn't the only one who knew it. We all felt it—the loss mixed with an awareness of the blessing that we ever knew her at all. Like every precious thing, her time with us was too fleeting, and it was a gift, like a perfect flower opening in the morning sun and wilting by nightfall.

An usher handed us programs. On the cover was a different photo of Leanna. This time, she was wearing my wedding pearls. The photo had been taken just six weeks before, at Christina's graduation. Later, Christina would share with me a treasured memory from that day.

———

It's an afternoon in late May when Leanna sets off in her car to help Christina dress for graduation. Normally, it would be an unremarkable occasion for me, but this day has been punctuated by sudden gusts of wind and rain, and Leanna has only been driving alone for two months. I hold my breath as she grabs her keys from the kitchen counter and races to her car, parked in the garage. "I can't be late, Mom," she exclaims.

"Okay, sweetheart! You look beautiful in that dress. I love the floral print on you." I holler after her. "Be careful in this rain! Text me when you get there."

"I will. I promise," she says with her silly grin.

Leanna arrives safely, runs through the puddles, and finds Christina in the ladies' bathroom, pacing back and forth. As the vice president of the senior class, she has to deliver a speech.

"Hey, Tina! I'm here—finally. Geez, it's pouring! I'm half-soaked," Leanna throws her arms around her friend then stands back to look at Christina in her orange graduation gown. "You're a pumpkin!" she says laughing. "The cutest pumpkin I ever did see!"

"Ha-ha. Thanks," Christina replies sarcastically. "Hey, can you help me with my cap? These things are so awkward. I can't get it to stay on right. Here, I have some bobby pins. And while you're doing that, I'm going to read over my speech one more time."

"Yes, read it aloud. I'll be your audience," Leanna smiles. "You're gonna be great tonight!"

As Leanna fixes the last of the pins, Christina sighs. "Leanna, what would I do without you?"

Leanna's hands drop to Christina's shoulders, and she gives them a squeeze, then looking her best friend in the eyes, says, "You'll never have to find out."

———

Clay asked the congregation to rise as Rogers, Steve, and I entered the sanctuary. We followed the usher to the front pew, and with hundreds of loving eyes on us, we took our places next to Steve's grandmother. Reverend Woody sat to my right and held my hand throughout the entire service. All around us, people continued to settle in, spilling into the fellowship hall and in the outside labyrinth. Large projector screens and loudspeakers were set up to reach those outside the main sanctuary. Later, someone told me more than a thousand people had come to honor Leanna.

Finally, the service began. After Clay's welcoming remarks, a collection of family and friends offered prayers, songs, and poems, doing their best to make the service as upbeat as a teenager's funeral could be. My sister, Tracy, rose to deliver a prayer. Hands on the pulpit, she steadied herself for a few moments, finally finding strength after shedding a few tears. Then it was Rogers's turn. He was solemn, but his eyes were dry. As he stood at the pulpit in his dark suit and bright red tie, he opened a Bible, took a long breath, then began to read. "The Lord is my shepherd I shall not want . . ." His voice steady and confident, he made it through Psalm 23 without a stumble or stutter. That is his way—to rise to the occasion—and to honor his beloved sister.

At one of my office visits with Caryn after Leanna's death, she described an experience she'd had with several of her clients. As someone who could tune into others' energy, Caryn had worked with many people through illness, grief, and loss. "During the time of death, something surrounds the person who is passing," she said, "like a spiritual portal, of sorts—a gateway that supports them and guides them through to the other side. It's hard to describe it exactly, but that portal extends to those closest to them too."

As I sat there on the front pew, taking it all in—the goodbyes, the music, and the prayers—I had yet to shed a tear and felt remarkably strong. Perhaps, as Caryn had described, I was being closely held in a space where I could handle or process all that was being doled out to me. But when the first few mysterious notes of Beethoven's "Moonlight Sonata" filled the sanctuary, emotion permeated every cell of my body. I reflected on a time, just six months before, when Leanna was sitting at the piano, playing the same piece. My mother was there, leaning on the piano and listening.

"Leanna," she said softly, "when I die, I would like for you to play this at my funeral."

Instead, Clay had arranged for one of the church staff to play it at Leanna's funeral.

Finally, it was time for Steve to speak. He squeezed my hand then stood and made his way to the pulpit, where he reached inside his pocket and pulled out his notes and his horn-rimmed reading glasses. Unfolding the paper, he cleared his throat, then began, his voice solemn but steady.

"If you came here today looking for explanations as to why, we cannot answer that call. As you might expect, we've rolled through that question in our minds a thousand times. The truth is that only God and Leanna know why. They have a plan, and over time, they will reveal it to us."

Finally, Clay got up and offered his eulogy, woven with love, faith, and light-hearted humor. He spoke of Leanna being home in her final resting place with God, of the mission work that was so important to her, and how in West Virginia, she found a place where she belonged. Clay also described Leanna's playfulness and how she loved to dance.

"We danced the last time we were together, at Vacation Bible School. And let me just warn you," Clay said with his trademark grin, "Presbyterians are typically known as the 'frozen chosen.'" The congregation laughed.

Clay then stepped away from the podium toward the communion table. He took off his white stole and blue robe, and in his white shirt, bow tie, and black pants, all six feet, two inches of Clay began to shimmy to a lively song, played by the church band, that was popular with the kids. "We call this dance an 'energizer,'" he said.

In a heartbeat, Rogers was on his feet, taking off his blazer and tossing it on the pew. Then Kate, another teen, followed. It wasn't in the program, and we hadn't planned it, but all over the church, folks stood and started dancing. In the pews, the aisles, and the balconies, we let our grief take flight. For a few cherished minutes, it was almost like the Coldplay concert, and once again, my heart felt a surge of joy from the soaring spirits that surrounded me.

As the congregation began to settle back down, Clay returned to the pulpit. "Thank you for joining me in honoring Leanna that way. And you honored her in life, as well. The last time I checked CaringBridge, there were more than 32,000 visits." He leaned into the microphone and said slowly, punctuating each word, "You loved her well."

Then, Reverend John Ross, who worked alongside Clay, rose to deliver the benediction. He reminded us of Leanna's passion for service and mission work. "She fought the good fight," he said. "She kept the faith." Slowly, he reached his arms wide and high, the fabric from his robe draping down and taking the shape of an angel's wings. "If you admire and love the things you have seen in Leanna's life, all that's been talked about, then you will get to know her God," he declared. "And so, I invite you. She will pass the baton on to you. It's your turn, my friends, to run the race with perseverance. Run the race that is set before you. In the name of Christ, take the baton and give witness, even as Leanna has given witness to us all."

With organ music filling the church, Steve, Rogers, and I rose from the pew and walked down the center aisle, followed by Reverend Woody and Clay. Everyone stood, watching as we passed. A few moments later, I looked up to see my mother crossing the threshold into the narthex. She held out her arms, and as she reached me, I fell gently into her embrace. Wordless, we stood there for long moments. She was struggling too. Unlike the first time my mother had arrived to be with me and comfort me on the loss of the child we never got a chance to know, this time, she felt the loss acutely. For my part, it was an experience beyond words for my mother to hold me in the face of grief over losing my daughter. It wasn't supposed to be this way.

Finally, my mother and I separated. Steve and Rogers were waiting for me, and as we turned toward the exit, an usher leaned against one of the big wooden doors, and we were washed in blinding bright light. There, with the sun beaming down, stood Dr. Everett. With a grateful heart, I ran to him. We quickly embraced as the mourners poured out of the sanctuary behind me.

"I'm so glad you came today," I whispered.

"It means a lot to be here," he replied solemnly.

Part of me wanted to stay behind and talk to Dr. Everett and the assembled crowd, but Clay pointed out that greeting so many people and managing their energy would be too much for us. Yet as we drove away, I felt the love of the hundreds who stood and stared.

The town car took us home for a quiet gathering of family and close friends. Once again, loved ones milled about, spoke in hushed tones, exchanged hugs. It was the type of gathering, drenched in empathy and understanding that I wish could happen in ordinary times; it was the type of event—with just dear loved ones—that emphasized a missing guest.

After I managed to eat small bites of marinated beef and grilled vegetables that Caryn had plated for me, I looked across the room, and my eyes landed on a lone figure seated on the purple sofa, his shoulders hunched. My father. As much as I had craved his attention and acceptance, he and I had not been close until I had started a family. Watching him there, I recalled a scene on another sofa many years ago.

——

I'm eleven years old, sitting in the den and watching TV when suddenly, I realize that everyone else is in the living room. Something serious is happening in there. I think, "If I walk over to the stairs, maybe they'll hear me and call me in." It works; they do.

As I enter the room, I notice how heavy it feels. I sit on a small, upholstered maroon-and-gold chair that has been in Mom's family forever. There are large picture windows at each end of that room, along with a brick fireplace. Dad is sitting on the long couch, slip-covered in blue-and-gold flowers, where he reads the Virginia Pilot. *Mom is in a chair next to the couch, her head bowed, a Kleenex in her hand.*

Dad looks up at me. "Beth, honey," he says, "I'm leaving home."

My throat hurts as I hold back tears; I know now that I will have no chance for a relationship with my father. All he cares about are fancy cars and showing off what a success he is. We don't matter to him. I sob in my seat then get up, walk over, and sit down next to my father on the couch.

He pauses awkwardly then puts his arm around me. He fumbles at the gesture; this is new for him. The prospect of leaving us seems to bring out something different in him, something approaching tenderness. "You'll always be my little girl," he says.

A few days later, Mom takes us all to Busch Gardens for the day while Dad packs up two closets full of clothes—all his silk ties and gold cufflinks and woolen slacks, every bit of the façade he shows the world—and moves out.

After Dad leaves, he hires a lawyer to work out child support payments—a "family friend." The lawyer draws up a document stating Dad should only pay $200 per month per child until we turn eighteen. That is all we will get to cover food, clothes, doctor bills, school fees . . . Mom had believed the lawyer was her friend, too, but soon enough, we realize we have been cheated. Mom works hard teaching school to span the gap that my father's leaving creates, both emotionally and financially, but there's only so much one person can do. His absence creates a hole in my life and in my heart.

———

It wasn't until Leanna was born that my father made a consistent effort to be a part of my life. Looking at him there on our sofa after her funeral, I knew that as much as he was there because of Leanna, he was there for me too. He had come to the hospital, was with us at church on Sunday, and as I stood and watched him, a single tear slid down his weathered cheek. It was the first time I ever saw my father cry.

In the time after Leanna's passing, my father continued to show up for my family and me. Visiting, staying in touch. It was likely because of her passing—now knowing too well how short life can truly be—that I was able to accept the belated gifts of his love and attention.

Somehow, after all those years, Leanna had answered my childhood prayer.

Chapter 16

During the first few weeks without Leanna, all I knew was that my life's journey had taken a tortuous turn into a dark, dismal cave. There was no roadmap to follow—no easy path to peace. I was blindfolded, having to feel my way out. In those days, I merely existed, with enough energy only to support and be present for my son and my husband. I questioned my reason for living; I questioned my faith in God. Feeling alone and abandoned, anxiety dominated my thoughts and made me believe I might never again see the light of day.

Steve, Rogers, and I managed to get up every morning, eventually finding a routine of sorts. Steve returned to his busy work schedule, and I managed the house and shuttled Rogers wherever he wanted to go. Driving Rogers around, preparing the family's meals, washing our clothes, walking the dogs—fulfilling these once mundane tasks gave me purpose. Even though our number was one fewer, care was still needed, and I could still provide it.

Yet Steve knew that home alone with my grief, I was vulnerable. I needed to surround myself with something solid—a task that would require more of my time and energy. He urged me to focus on the fundraising projects that were coming up in the fall, that doing something for others would keep me from becoming swallowed by my own sense of loss.

As the kids got older and spent more time at school and their extra-curricular activities, I began to seek other ways to be of use. For three years straight, I served as the gala chair for a local non-profit.

For one of these events, The Night of Hope Gala, as I began planning and fundraising, Leanna showed an interest in what I was up to.

———

"I have an idea," I say. "I am thinking about putting together a kids' committee to help with the gala. Would you like to be on it?"

"Wow, really?" she smiles. "Sure!"

It is just the reassurance I need.

Rogers joins as well, and they get to see not only what's involved in plan-ning and pulling off such an event, but also experience a sense of purpose and the satisfaction that comes from giving back. One thing I'd always noticed in my life was that whatever questions I'd had about who I was and why I was here, in moments of serving others, there were no questions—just pure contentment.

The night of the gala, we all dress up. I wear a long navy gown speckled with sequins. Leanna graces an adorable yet sophisticated look, wearing a black and white strapless cocktail dress with bright red heels that sparkle like Dorothy's ruby slippers. Rogers and Steve sport dark suits and ties with pressed white shirts.

As we enter the event room just before the guests arrive, Leanna stops and looks around. The theme for the gala is "Over the Moon." The room is draped in navy satin, from curtains to tablecloths, and bathed in ambient light. Atop each table is a centerpiece of white orchids lit from beneath to create an ethereal glow. Perfectly printed programs rest on each plate. A live band plays softly in the background with a full moon drawn by a local art student serving as their backdrop. "Mom," Leanna says as she sits down next to me, her eyes wide as she continues to notice the details. "I am so proud of you."

———

Steve was right. It was helpful for me to start thinking about this year's gala, listing out all that would need to be done. It was something to keep me busy, but it also provided an opportunity to think about someone other than myself. Ironically, the organization we were raising money for provided psychosocial support for patients with cancer and their families. During our time in the hospital, I'd gotten to see first-hand just how crucial those services are. While we had the love and support of so many family members and friends, some of whom took time from work to be with us, not everyone is fortunate enough to have such resources.

During that first week after Leanna's death and the weeks that followed, Steve relied on the distraction of the office to get through each day. On weekends, I'd hear him clanging around in the kitchen, chopping vegetables as he half-watched baseball on the TV. His strategy for dealing with the pain was to bury it by staying busy, which I later learned is much harder than talking about it.

The Sunday after Leanna's service, at Steve's suggestion, we hosted a gathering of friends. Steve proposed that we have a guacamole competition.

"A what?" I squinted at him.

"You know, like a chili cookoff but with guacamole. Best batch wins."

I stared at him. "You want to have sixteen people over for a guacamole competition? Today?" I said, thinking perhaps hearing it repeated would help him realize the lunacy of the idea.

Instead, he nodded. "Yeah, what do you think? I mean, I know it's a lot, but it will help us get our mind off of things for a few hours."

"*Get our mind off of things?*" I said, incredulous at the idea that anything on this earth could redirect my mind from the loss of our daughter.

Running from grief is the worst game of hide-and-seek, constantly searching out places you hope that grief can't find you. Steve was having more trouble than he could admit, and it would take him years to realize he needed help. It's easy to assume that he would have had an easier time had he faced his demons earlier, but there's also a divine plan at play, and sometimes things take the time and course they're meant to. It certainly seemed like divine intervention, or perhaps an angel named Leanna, was involved when Steve finally did seek therapy.

In contrast, my struggle was more evident in the first days and weeks after Leanna's death, but my willingness to be present with my grief served me well. There is no way to make grief easy, as I've found, but when we allow it to do its work rather than stifle it, we can begin to access a sense of peace.

Many years after Leanna's passing, I watched a TED Talk by a remarkable couple named Mark Pollock and Simone George. When the couple met, Mark was blind. After a freak accident during which Mark fell from a three-story window, he became paralyzed. The two spoke about how to balance acceptance and hope, and one line in particular from Simone struck me: "Acceptance is knowing that grief is a raging river, and you have to get into it because when you do, it carries you to the next place; it eventually takes you to open land, somewhere where it will turn out okay in the end."

By then I knew from my own experience the truth of this insight. After Leanna passed, I stepped into the river, eventually letting it take me, while Steve, who was used to being in charge, continued for years to struggle against the current. During the typical workweek, after a full day, he'd walk in the door around 6:00 p.m. I couldn't read his face to know how his day had been. I knew he was trying to stay steady for us, but it often felt like my husband was absent. An hour after dinner, he was asleep on the purple couch, the Cardinals game droning on in the background. On weekends, cooking continued to be his refuge. The recipes he chose were absurdly elaborate with their many carefully timed steps and special ingredients, allowing Steve to become lost in the complexity of his creations.

———

Meanwhile, I was desperate for some sense of contact with Leanna. I kept her toiletries in a little black case and even used her toothbrush for a while. I preserved her tube of toothpaste because it still held the imprint of her hand. They had been hers, and so these everyday items took on infinite value. I couldn't bear to throw them out. Her most common possessions became extraordinary to me. I wore her pink and gray wristwatch until it stopped working.

Is this how it's done? I thought to myself. *Is this how a parent grieves the loss of a child?*

As I drove Rogers to crew practice or to meet with friends, I began to wonder if kids grieve differently from adults. When I looked at his smiling face, I sometimes questioned if they grieve at all, though I believe they do. Still, none of us is born with a preconceived notion of loss or how to handle it—not on a conscious level, anyway. For better or worse, perhaps we learn it over time, by watching others. I suppose that's why cultural influence is so strong. While our culture is largely one that suppresses grief, other cultures view death as a natural part of life, where grief is expressed openly, and sadness and gratitude are welcomed together.

With Rogers carrying on with his life, no doubt he missed Leanna, but he didn't let sadness stop him. "I have crew practice this morning until nine, then I'm going to Panera with a few friends," he reported. "After that, I'm going ice skating up in Palmetto with Liz—she's in town for a few days." Rogers had never experienced the loss of a loved one until now, so in my mind, he provided a pure example of how to go forward.

He was responding to an instinct that seemed to say, "Keep on living. Don't complicate it. Just keep *living*!"

Oh, I thought, *so that's how it's done.*

Rogers was both teaching me how to go on and providing me with the means of doing so. Like other parents, I'd done my share of complaining about running "Mom's taxi," but now I welcomed the diversion. It was also an opportunity to let Rogers know, as best I could, that I was there for him. That grief had not swallowed me whole.

Although he pursued life tasks with uncanny cheer, after Leanna's death, Rogers did become quieter; it seemed a lot of his processing, too, was internal. At some point, I had a small wallet-sized print made for him of a photo of Leanna and him at the beach. She was six years old, and he was three, and they were side by side, holding hands. Leanna was looking down at Rogers, who was staring off into the distance. "She's always here for you, Rogers, watching over you," I said as I handed the photo to him. "Let this be a reminder."

I was comforted by the fact that Rogers was spending time with his friends and his girlfriend and seemed to be having fun. I didn't know if he was opening up to them or not; I hoped he was. But I didn't want to push him or intrude. I learned that the hard way. The few times I attempted to ask how he was doing with his feelings, he shut down immediately. So I dropped it. I didn't want him to pull away from me. I did, however, insist on one thing: that he attend therapy.

"Okay, Mom, but I don't think I need to," Rogers said in the car on the way to the grocery store.

"Rog, I'm not going to go in with you, and I'm not even going to tell you what to talk about. But I want you to go to three sessions with a therapist. That's all I ask. After that, you can keep going, or you can decide that's it and you're done."

He was quiet for a few moments. "Three?"

"Three."

Rogers sighed. "Okay."

I never asked Rogers what he discussed. During his sessions, I simply sat in the waiting room reading one of my books on grieving. Afterward, he'd come out, I'd rise and give him a hug, and we'd head home. He never opted to return after the third session, but here and there over the years, I've casually mentioned that the offer of therapy was still good if he ever wanted to go back.

———

During quiet moments, I began to confront the fact that I had to accept that Leanna's physical life on earth was over. Life had to go on; I couldn't allow myself to become frozen by what had happened. *Just keep moving*, that little voice kept saying. I took the dogs for long walks and drove to three different hot yoga studios hoping the heat would melt away my misery as it had so many years ago when Steve and I had lost our first child.

Oddly, or perhaps not, it wasn't until I took on the considerable task of writing this book that I linked the two—the loss of our first baby before she'd even had a chance to live and of Leanna. When Leanna's earthly life ended, I didn't think of myself as a mother who had lost her second child. It was only as I looked back on the story of my life that I made the connection. Truth be told, because of how the fetus had developed with neither distinctly male nor female characteristics, I had never thought of our first baby as a girl. It was when I traveled back to these spaces, hoping to make enough sense of them, that I discovered Turner syndrome is only present in females. That's how life is, with old stories taking on new shades as distance sheds light on them.

Then, as I shared early drafts of this book with others, one reader keyed in on our first loss and realized that she, too, had unresolved grief from a pregnancy that did not end in a live birth. It is yet another thing

I have learned about how we handle loss; that when we don't process our feelings—when we downplay or are not fully present with our grief—it lies in wait for us until we have the awareness and resources to acknowledge it. Or, in some cases, until another series of events, a shift in the universe, some element of God's plan, or whatever force unearths it and places it, bare and shivering, before us.

Each of these experiences has emphasized the essential nature of grief—how it is so tightly woven into our lives that to ignore it is to wall off entire parts of ourselves. To leave large pieces of our lives unlived. Instead of letting the river take us and deposit us somewhere new, we live these half-lives where some part of us is always fighting the current.

Years after Leanna's passing, as I watched the world struggle to navigate the coronavirus pandemic, I wondered if this event we seemed so powerless to stop was, in part, a global exercise in shifting the way we grieve. As people felt their lives crumbling around them, I stood calm, as if in the eye of the storm, simply observing. It's not as though the pandemic didn't affect me, but by having a new perspective on death, I found it almost impossible to be shaken as deeply as others seemed to be. That, too, was a gift of floating down the river of grief—finding my true resolve and my deeper reason for being here. But *first*, I had to let myself be carried by the current.

Chapter 17

For at least six weeks, sleep was my biggest challenge. Steve and I both leaned on Xanax for help. The medication made me less anxious, took off some of the edge, and helped me complete each day—to release my mind and fall asleep. In the morning, I'd wake up groggy, my senses dulled, with no urge to get up and do anything. I didn't know if my numbness was the pain of loss, a side effect of the Xanax, or both. I wished for a magic potion that could help me relax and sleep but be gone from my system when I awoke.

As we sat in bed at night, Steve and I would check in with one another. "How much are you taking tonight?" It was a tangible way to measure some small progress in our grieving. When I began to feel a little stronger, I started to cut back on the Xanax—half a pill a night, then a quarter of a pill. Eventually, I was free of it altogether.

During those weeks, I tried dozens of ways of coping, some of which led me down proverbial rabbit holes. Once the Xanax was out of my system, I became keenly aware of which methods worked for me and which didn't. I started to realize that I'd have to choose my means of support carefully.

As I fumbled through those early days, I began to learn the importance of preserving and protecting my energy. While love poured in from friends and family around me, some individuals became especially needy. As time went on, I learned to be more discerning by listening to my intuition. When certain people wanted to engage with me, I simply declined, saying as kindly as I could that I needed to rest or that it just wasn't a good time. Sometimes, I truly didn't have the energy to be with anyone and was doing my best just to keep breathing. I needed to focus on staying calm and getting as much precious sleep as I could. To that end, every time I lay down to try to rest, I taped a sign to the door asking not to be disturbed. Sleep was a rare and precious commodity and my escape from reality. On those rare occasions when I was able to nap, I guarded silence like a Navy SEAL, commanding quiet. I instructed visitors to please come back another time and delivery drivers to simply leave packages and go.

I began to take notes on these and other discoveries as if I was on a special mission. One thing I realized was that the simplest gestures were often the most profound. One morning, a few days after Leanna's service, my phone lit up. It was a text from Greg, who had already done so much for us. I tapped my phone to see a picture of a brilliant sunrise, along with the words, "I'm thinking of you." Every few days for months, Steve and I received a similar text from Greg—always something brief, just letting us know we were not forgotten. That we were not alone.

Another tactic that helped our family was to get away from the house more—to break up the patterns of our lives. Leanna's absence was palpable; we needed to create something new. We couldn't change the fact that Leanna was no longer with us in human form, but we could take trips away from the house and all the memories it held. Our first outing was to New York City. Steve and I flew with Rogers and a friend up for a few days to experience an environment that was a total three-sixty from our everyday life at home. The distances may not matter much; driving ten miles to the next town might have worked just as well. Either way, we found travel to be a blessed diversion, especially over Thanksgiving,

Christmas, and other major holidays, with the new surroundings providing an opportunity to shift our mindsets.

Grief is so disorienting and uncomfortable that it frequently makes people awkward. Not knowing what to say, they would sometimes utter wince-inducing phrases such as, *She's in a better place* or someone's suggestion that, at forty-eight, I have another baby. But what felt better were simple declarations and gestures. *I love you. I'm praying for you. Would you like me to come sit with you for a while?* And instead of asking vague questions—such as, *What can I do for you?*—bringing us a meal and asking when it might be convenient to drop it off was far more helpful and required less mental effort on our part. I will also add that the love and affection of our dogs were particularly helpful, and perhaps, a pet could provide some extra support in the aftermath of loss.

Longtime friends, such as Vidisha, waited for a time when our out-of-town relatives had returned home—when quiet pervaded the house again—before reaching out. She came to the house and simply sat with me. I recalled the time when she and I joked about her son, Chetan, kissing Leanna when they were young and how we were going to remind them about that when their senior prom rolled around. Now, Leanna would never go to senior prom.

When you've lost a child, you can tell your friends about it, but they can't say, "Yes, I've felt that too." You are left in a lonely place where you have to rely on yourself to get through. In those early days, I was desperate to talk to another mother who had lost a child. I needed to know whether it was possible to find peace again. Steve and I were in our own private nightmare, afraid of being trapped forever. I had to know if there was any hope.

The second Sunday after Leanna's death, Steve, Rogers, and I gathered in the church library. Across from us sat a woman in her early forties. Her expression was somber but kind. I had asked her to meet with us, and she was kind enough to agree. Years before, she had lost her six-year-old daughter to brain cancer.

"Thank you for meeting with us," I said. She offered a slight smile and a nod. "My one burning question, I hope you can answer . . . I just have to know . . ." I paused to take a steadying breath. "Will we ever have peace again?"

Her reply was quiet and succinct. "Yes, you will have peace again."

With two other young children, she had moved forward with her life. In honor of her daughter, she started a foundation to raise money for pediatric cancer research. And while the success of that foundation helped to ease the pain and find purpose in her loss, she admitted that she had not yet been able to hang the most recent family portrait in her home because Riley, her daughter, was not in it.

That she had found peace was reassuring, but I also found comfort in her honesty and the fact that she still grieved her daughter. While I longed for a day when I would be relieved of acute suffering, I was also afraid of moving on too far.

———

I shied away from support groups despite the encouragement of others to do so. My intuition didn't buy into group therapy at the time. Would I be cast at sea with a group of people whose ship had just sunk? What if in their own floundering and struggle to be saved, they pulled me down with them?

Steve and I did try counseling with an individual therapist, and though it felt right to try to do *something,* the session was yet another tough lesson in managing grief. While desperate for concrete advice or techniques to ease our pain, we sat there on the couch, facing the counselor surveying us from his padded armchair, and his first words were some of the least helpful I have ever heard. "You are living my worst nightmare." I may have outwardly cringed when he said that. Then, he sat there in his navy blazer and pressed khakis, forearms resting atop the armrests, as though his job was to simply let us vent. Angry and frustrated, we gave up after one session. In retrospect, I would have asked for a recommendation for a counselor from a trusted friend. As it was, the therapist was someone we had found on the internet, and we had spent a precious, energetic coin on a losing bet.

Now in my continued efforts to try to shift the paradigm of grief support for myself and others, I often seek the company of parents, especially mothers, who have experienced the loss of a child. Usually, it's one-on-one, but about eight years after Leanna passed, one day, I had a strong notion of gathering these mothers to remember some of the beautiful things about their child or children. By that point, I'd met and talked with a lot of them. As I discovered, mothers who have lost children seem to have a way of finding one another. Wanting to set a positive tone right away, I invited close to twenty women to a restaurant for lunch and, if they felt like it, to share some happy memories of their children. Most came and, as we sat around a large table in a private room, these mothers could *clearly* see that they were not alone in their loss. There was laughter, fellowship, and tears—mostly tears of joy. That's another thing I've learned: While we do need spaces to share our sorrow and our grief, it's as important to share the joy and gratitude these beautiful beings brought into our lives.

Though a grief support group was the last place I wanted to be, in retrospect, it might have also been my introverted personality that made me shy away from groups. Perhaps people who are more extroverted and naturally draw strength and energy from the presence of others would be more inclined to participate. I might have benefitted from the right group at the time, but it's impossible to know. In some ways, grief affects us similarly, but in others, our experiences are unique. I had hoped, at the time, for some kind of road map. I understand now that there is none. Some strategies, like support groups and grief counselors, help many people, but no strategy helps everyone. Now I tell people, if you attend a support group and it does not feel right to you, don't hesitate to excuse yourself. Listen to your inner guide. Your gut feelings are important; they will help lead you down the path that is best for your recovery.

As outgoing as he can be, Steve is an introvert as well. Neither of us expresses big emotional displays or exchanges, yet the depth and feelings are there. Perhaps, for this reason, a few quiet rituals we developed to honor and remember Leanna became great sources of comfort. One of the rituals started with no big pronouncement. In the early days of our grief, when Steve, Rogers, and I were sitting down to dinner, one of us—I can't remember who—said, "Let's start lighting a candle every night for Leanna." Still, to this day at dinnertime, Steve or I will light that candle. At some point, our dog, Lucie, began coming over at dinnertime and flopping down in Leanna's empty space. That was her ritual for a very long time. Such gestures are small, but their meaning and impact are great.

As I grieved Leanna, another lifeline I reached for was books about grieving, with differing results. I leafed through most of the books people offered but put them down when they failed to show me a better way of looking at loss. Books had always been companions of mine, and in hard times, maps of the terrain. But some of these authors, it seemed, attempted to fit my entire ocean of pain and baffled anger into a few shallow categories and stages. There was a false certitude about it all. As I understand now, while we might hope in our darkest moments for some mathematical formula to solve the problem of our pain, it's the uniqueness of our journeys—ones we must learn to walk for ourselves—that reveals to us what is there. And the person we lost was not like anyone else in this world, nor are we, so it makes no sense to think that our ways forward would share the same path.

One book I picked up that was recommended by another grieving parent included a chapter on the death of a child. I turned to it immediately, desperate for some comfort. It read along the lines of "poor you— we understand how devasted you are. Not only are you grieving the death of your child, you are also grieving that he or she will never graduate from high school or college and will never get married or have children."

I slammed the book shut. *How dare you!* I thought. *I hadn't even thought of those scenarios, and here you are adding to my sorrow!* I threw the book onto the bed, never to open it again.

Often, words failed me as I navigated the haze of grief. As one of my friends said, there are aspects of grief that are deeply connected to our subconscious, in territories that are literally beyond language. When we mine our thoughts for meaning and sense, we're often left empty-handed. That's part of the reason I've written this book now—to find the words I didn't have back in 2012 and to paint the bigger picture that, in those early days, I could not yet see.

Chapter 18

Soldiers who have lost arms and legs in battle insist they still have feeling there, though the limb is gone. I felt like that with Leanna. She was gone from me physically, but her voice and gestures, the smell of her shampoo, or the sound of her voice would come to me at odd times. It was painful on one hand, but my biggest fear was that these memories would fade, along with my sense of her presence. I was terrified of forgetting her laugh, her silly grin, and the dozens of little jokes we shared.

By the same token, thoughts of Leanna sometimes led me right to what happened to her and the crushing knowledge that Steve and I had been helpless to stop it. In those early days, it was dangerous to spend too much time with memories and thoughts that didn't serve me, like staring too long at the sun.

So, I continued looking for distractions and ways to take care of myself. I set little goals: get some physical activity every day; set aside time for sleep or other rest; work on the gala. Steve continued to stay busy with work, buying himself time before confronting his devastation. Because we were grieving in parallel, I was desperate to find something he and I could do together to both occupy our minds and bring us together.

We signed up for a series of ballroom dancing lessons but stopped when we couldn't find a rhythm. As Clay said, the "frozen chosen…" Instead, we relied on our love of cooking to bring us together and enjoyed nice dinners at home.

———

Following Leanna's funeral and for many weeks later came the cards. Every day brought more of them, and after the first week, I found I could not read one more word of sympathy. I gave myself permission to stop reading them, opening each card only to see who it was from and whether it included a check. In Leanna's obituary, we identified three organizations where people could donate if they wished. Of great comfort was knowing these groups would receive some support in her honor.

The pile of cards on the kitchen counter grew daily until it looked as if one or two more might send it toppling over. Finally, I tucked them in a small box, thinking I would read them later. They remain untouched in the corner of Leanna's bedroom, yet I'm glad I kept them. Just seeing them is still a visual reminder that people were thinking of us.

One day, along with the usual stack of cards, the mail lady delivered a small cardboard box to our door. As I reached out to accept the package, our eyes met. "I'm so sorry for your loss," she said.

I nodded. "Thank you."

Sometimes, when people are afraid to mention your loss, it's in part, because they worry that their words will bring it to mind, as if somehow, for a moment, you might have forgotten. I have *always* appreciated any form of acknowledgment and *always* will. Having a loved one remembered, no matter how small the gesture, is *everything*.

I took the package inside and to the kitchen. Intrigued by the box, I reached for a knife and cut the packing tape. Inside, carefully wrapped in brown paper, was a small replica of the Golden Gate Bridge. A note revealed that it was a gift from Steve's high-school friend, Jeff. The letter Jeff included was humble and eloquent and explained that he used images or structures to channel his feelings. To him, a bridge was a symbol of how we could get from here to there and stay above troubled water.

I turned the replica over in my hands. *We are suspended between two worlds*, I thought. It was a message that spoke to me. I placed the bridge on the counter, where it remained, prominently displayed, for months—a reminder that we were being ushered by God to the other side. Even now, when I see it, that message is renewed for me.

I began to see Caryn at her office twice a week instead of my typical once a month. As I lay down on the table in her office and the acupuncture needles went in, I met my terror head-on. My heart fluttered then pounded as I felt my fear and anxiety crescendo to sharp peaks, then drop into dark valleys.

Faith and trust, I reminded myself. *Faith and trust.* I let myself surf the waves, never feeling complete relief, but allowing them to guide me where they would. Something about the surrender, the relinquishing of the illusion of control—riding that river of grief—was its own strange comfort.

One day, I came into Caryn's office with my mind going in a terrible direction. As I lay on the massage table, Caryn gently inserted the needles. With tears streaming down my face, I told her what that book for grieving parents had said and how angry and betrayed I'd felt.

"Now, Leanna will never graduate from high school or college. She will never get married or have children," I sobbed. "I wanted support; instead I got a kick in the stomach."

Caryn was quiet for a moment. "Beth," her gentle voice sounded, "how do you know Leanna would have done any of those things anyway?"

I lay there and let her words sink in. She was right. As parents, we have grand dreams for our children, but they are *our* dreams. Many of them never turn out as we had envisioned, even if our children are alive and well. We get so angry because a child's death seems so untimely—so *wrong*. These things are not "supposed" to happen. No, we are all "supposed" to fall in love, have children, then live fulfilling, untroubled lives. Yet, when does that ever happen? Losing a child is a grief unlike any other, yet as I've heard many different teachers say, the degree to which we suffer over a loss corresponds to the degree to which we fail to accept that loss, to insist that it was not supposed to happen. And yet, how are we to know what is supposed to happen?

We make death and grief into something to be ignored until it's forced upon us, even though for every one of us, it is inevitable. Nothing will ever make a loss, especially the loss of a child, *feel* okay, especially in the beginning. It is *torture*. But there is a greater context—a greater story being told—and we see only pieces of it at a time. The reality was that I had no idea what Leanna's story would be had she lived a full life, but I had pretended to know by constructing one of my own.

I realized, lying there on Caryn's table, that was *my* story, not Leanna's. We couldn't know Leanna's story, as we don't know any of our stories until they are lived. And in her case, and perhaps it's the case for all of us, her story would continue to unfold even after her passing.

———

Six weeks after Leanna died, I read on social media about the tragic news of another local family who lost a teen. Without thinking about it and even surprising myself a little, I sent the family a message. In it, I described briefly what we were going through and did my best to offer a sense that things will get better. I wanted to pass on the gift that the woman from church had given me. I expressed that even though I had a long way to go, it was already a little bit easier to get through the days.

I never heard back from the family, and that's okay. Even if they didn't see my message, I know in my heart they still *received* it.

—

Three months after Leanna's death, I felt like I was ready to go through her things. I hadn't touched any of them since she had died. I knew it would be easier on Steve if I handled it, but I knew I wasn't up to doing it alone. But who could I ask? A name popped into my head—Hillary. She had been one of Leanna's elementary school teachers, and we had kept in touch. Hillary was kind and a devoted teacher, and while she had known Leanna well, she didn't have the same emotional attachment as a family member so I reasoned that the task might not be as much of a burden to her.

"Of course, I'd be honored to help," Hillary said. One afternoon, a short time later, she came to the house, sat with me on Leanna's bedroom floor, and helped me sort through my daughter's clothes, shoes, jewelry, and backpacks. Together, we arranged them into three piles—keep, throw out, and give away.

—

Little by little, there began to appear in my dark, dismal cave a tiny sliver of light. One evening, several months into our loss, Steve and I sat at the kitchen counter, having dinner. There was nothing remarkable about that day or that moment, but suddenly, out of nowhere, a mysterious feeling began to wash over me. My body warmed. I felt the hair on my arms and the back of my neck raise. It was as if my heart, grown so heavy these last few months, felt lighter. Every cell in my body breathed a moment of total, utter calm.

At the time, I had no idea what was happening. Now, I know that what I felt was the pure presence and gift of grace. A moment of true clarity.

I turned to Steve. My voice firm with conviction, I declared, "We are going to be okay. We are going to get through this." I knew it with everything in me.

Wordless, we held one another's gaze, and something passed between us. Our souls exchanged a new truth. The knowing that had been given to me was somehow transferred to Steve. I could see it in his eyes. We *were* going to be okay.

I felt my heart soften and slightly open to receive the support that had always been there, waiting. My faith was returning, only something felt different. It was as if there was a kind of new knowledge deep inside me that was mysterious and hard to name, preparing to unfold.

Years later, I heard Caroline Myss describe grace as a subtle and deeply mystical force that soothes and calms and profoundly shifts something inside you. I believe now that this is what I experienced in that pivotal moment.

From that night, what started as a trickle of love and faith began to permeate my being. I was finally moving forward. Whereas I had been pushing and dragging myself along from day to day, it now felt as if something was pulling me forward. It felt *hopeful*.

I'm not sure why that shift happened when it did. Perhaps it was because just before that, I had been thinking a lot about the Serenity Prayer, which I had memorized when I was ten.

May God grant me the serenity to accept the things I cannot change, the courage to change the things I can, and the wisdom to know the difference.

I realized that I wasn't sorting Leanna's clothes anymore; I was sorting my options, separating those things I could change from those I couldn't. Maybe that realization was a bridge. The first of many I would cross in the coming months.

———

I thought more and more about how we might remember Leanna

in a tangible, permanent way. I felt it would help me heal to start a memorial project for her, but I had no idea of the scale. Should we have a bench made and placed somewhere in our yard or do something bigger? I knew I wanted it to be a symbol of the change she had worked for in her short life.

The image that came to me was that of a fish. It is a symbol of Christianity and a reminder of the mission work so important to Leanna. We decided to have a sculpture made and placed it in our backyard. I also recognize that the fish is a powerful swimmer, adept in water, able to ride the waves and currents.

Often, I sit and meditate or pray where the sculpture rests nestled among the palm trees on a wood pedestal. One day not long after we had it installed, I ventured out to sit by the sculpture, I stopped in my tracks, unable to comprehend right away what I was seeing. As the sun filtered through the trees, the mixture of light and shadow cast the illusion of an eye and a mouth onto the fish. Not just a mouth, but one curved into a silly, sweet little grin.

———

I continued to practice yoga as best I could, knowing it would soothe my soul and bring me moments of peace. The waves of pain still sometimes felt insurmountable, but they began to come farther apart, with more time between them to catch my breath. In my mind and in my body, I could feel myself getting stronger. And I knew deep inside that some part of me was growing, like a dormant seed that had begun to sprout.

I went walking, I ate mindfully to sustain my body and my spirit, and I prayed. I needed my faith again—to believe in the presence of things I couldn't see and to trust that I was loved and held by God.

Chapter 19

In those moments when my heart rate slowed and my breathing became less shallow, I'd think, "Maybe this is it. Maybe I'm really climbing out," and then I would slip back to a place of pain and suffering. Grief is like that. The emotional storms can happen when you least expect them, often triggered by a song, a smell, or even a vibrant sunset. Knocked down again, I'd search for a new book or teaching—*anything* to give me comfort.

Yet even in those periods of pain and confusion, bits of certainty began to coalesce into a few things I knew for sure. The first was that Leanna's life and purpose hadn't ended when she left this earth; they were just beginning. I used to think that we live in our bodies, and we die when those bodies fail, sending our souls to heaven, but it became clear to me after Leanna's passing that this, alone, does not define us. We are all so much more than that.

I also knew that during Leanna's last days and the days that followed her death, many who knew her were profoundly moved by the entire experience. Friends, colleagues, and acquaintances admitted that, for the first time, they had begun to pray. As much as Leanna's death devastated all of us, I believe that something mystical happened in this space we had all shared. The surgeon felt it, along with the cardiologist, the intensivist, and the entire surgical staff. Even in our collective struggle and sadness—and perhaps because of it—a radiance enveloped us, and we were changed. Dr. Everett keeps a photo of Leanna taped to his computer.

Those who knew Leanna were left in awe by her energetic spirit, her infectious enthusiasm, and the overall beauty of her life. On some level, grace tells me that the One from which she came chose this path for her. And in some way, a different outcome for Leanna would have created a different outcome for us all.

And there was something else I grew to believe. Stephanie, one of Leanna's rowing friends, told me in the weeks after Leanna's passing that the eight-person boat just wasn't the same without her. Then she shared with me something that further fueled my hunch that on some level, Leanna knew that her time on earth would be short.

"I thought you should see this," Stephanie said. I looked down to see her holding a handmade card with a familiar flair, "It's the card Leanna gave me on her last Christmas," she said as I opened it.

Inside, I saw Leanna's handwriting, and at the very bottom it read: *Love me forever and I'll never leave you.*

In the ever-shifting world of teenagers, so obsessed with the present, Leanna had gifted Stephanie in advance with a message from eternity.

While I felt for footholds, searching for anything to help me climb out of the dark places, a sign would appear—a rainbow, a sudden sunlit smile on a stone fish, or a card like this one—letting us know that Leanna's love was still, and always will be, with us.

———

As I struggled to navigate my new life, a resource found me, perhaps with Leanna's help, that was both practical and spiritual. *Finding Inner Courage* is a book written by Mark Nepo, a writer, teacher, philosopher, and poet who survived cancer. Not focused on death per se, it is about all of life's trials and tribulations—and how we can find the strength to stand up to them. Reading this book first was a good choice because in those early days, I didn't want to be reminded of a loss I already knew too well.

Following *Finding Inner Courage*, I started to think more about what Leanna went through, what she saw and felt when she crossed over. I was filled with a need, an insatiable hunger, to read anything I could that might help me to know what my daughter experienced. Books on grief and near-death experiences had started to pile up in my office like the condolence cards on the kitchen counter. In that stack of books, I found *Proof of Heaven*, written by a neurosurgeon who had a brush with the afterlife. For seven days, the author, Dr. Eben Alexander, was in a coma. I found great comfort that during those seven days, Alexander described seeing heaven and experiencing profound love, connecting with a guardian angel, and speaking with the divine. To those who would say he was dreaming, Dr. Alexander points out that when we're in a coma, the cortex isn't functional. We do not dream. Alexander's descriptions buoyed my hope that in her passing, Leanna was free from all worldly concerns and held in pure love.

For his part and despite my nudging, Steve had no desire to read books on grief. Yet he did find his own way to peace by leaning on something larger. Some nights, I would wake from my own restless sleep, knowing he'd pray the rosary, alternating the Lord's Prayer and the Hail Mary if he needed comfort, even in the dark of the night. Eventually, Steve received his own visit from an angel, this one on earth.

In the summer of 2012, Cardinal Mooney—Steve's parochial high school—was throwing a fortieth reunion party for its 1972 state-champion football team. We had planned to host the party at our home but bowed out when Leanna fell ill. When Father Gerry Finegan, a former chaplain at Cardinal Mooney, heard about Leanna's passing, he would stop by the house to pray with us. There weren't many people who just dropped by after Leanna's death, which was a blessing, but Father Gerry's visits were always welcome. He radiated love and warmth and seeing him reconnected Steve to his Catholic roots.

One evening, Father Gerry joined us for dinner. As he entered our home and walked into the kitchen, he held out a book of his own to add to my collection.

"I brought this. I pray it brings you peace," he said in his soft Irish accent. "It's written by a theology professor, Jerry Sittser, who lost his wife, mother, and four-year-old daughter from a terrible car accident. He talks openly about his journey through grief."

My chest constricted. While desperate to read anything that might ease my suffering, why would I want to expose myself to such tragedy? I was afraid that this terrible story would add to my despair. "Thank you," I managed to say, my heart racing.

As he held out the book, I reached for the small, hardcover volume. Scanning its jacket, I read the title, *A Grace Disguised.* Right away, I pictured myself placing it on the bottom of my pile to read some other time, perhaps many years in the future. Or maybe never. But then, as I read the subtitle, my eyes grew wide. *How the Soul Grows Through Loss.* "Wait. *Grow?*" I asked myself.

My God! I thought. *Could there possibly be something positive to glean from this horror?* If so, I had to know what it was. Holding the book in my hands, I felt this deep sense—a kind of knowing that it just might *save* me.

As soon as Father Gerry left, I hurried to my bedroom, propped some pillows on the bed, and with a yellow highlighter in hand, began to read.

I absorbed Sittser's words, his feeling "dizzy with grief's vertigo, cut off from family and friends, tormented by the loss, nauseated from the pain." *Yes!* I thought. *Here is someone who truly knows what I'm feeling—*

and knows how to write about it. His story and reflections drew me in, and I was able to bear the sadness of his heartbreaking loss because, alongside it, he offered hope and a *positive* perspective on loss. The path before me was now illuminated.

Sittser explained that major loss is something you never get over. Instead, it brings with it a grief that you build into your *new* life. There is no hiding and no way out . . . but only through. I shuddered to read these key words: "You cannot outrun the darkness;" that, in order to get past the pain, I must *be* with it. I couldn't just sweep it all under the rug and expect it to go away.

As my soul rejoiced in the hopeful prose of *A Grace Disguised*, my highlighter found these words: "It is not what happens *to* us that matters so much as what happens *in* us," suggesting that we can *transcend* our suffering and *transform* our lives. He wrote that the soul can grow through suffering and that, " . . . once enlarged, the soul is also capable of experiencing greater joy, strength, peace, and love."

Wow, I thought. *This* is where I want to be.

I had found a new direction and by seeing death in a new way, I was then able to lead Steve and Rogers in a new direction too. We were all saved by this one sacred story.

A few months later, I read Thornton Wilder's *The Bridge of San Luis Rey*. Our friend John, who had given it to us, told us it had been a special book in his life after his little sister had drowned in a lake. Wilder tells the story of five travelers in Peru who fall to their death when a well-constructed bridge gives way. The theme is that when bodily life is gone, love remains, creating an enduring bridge to the soul of the person who departed.

Upon finishing that book, I reflected on bridges I had seen since Leanna became sick. There was CaringBridge, my connection to our faithful supporters and their prayers. And there was the replica of the Golden Gate Bridge that Jeff had sent us.

What struck me most, though, was my memory of Tropical Storm Debby. As Leanna was in crisis and the surgeon installed the LVAD to support her heart, Debby flooded large parts of Florida and caused the closing of the Sunshine Skyway Bridge. As Leanna struggled, storm clouds gathered low over the hospital. The sky was a wet blanket, heavy and dark, bearing down on us. Fierce winds blew, the rain came and went—slow one moment then at the next, pouring down in sheets. The following day, the skies cleared, Leanna was stable, and the bridge re-opened. The weight of the world, it seemed, had lifted, and I was surrounded by a new and expectant waiting with renewed hope.

This imagery of bridges became a pattern, a distinct message from God. And as the days went on, I found it unshakeable. Finally, when I received the Thornton Wilder book, it dawned on me, like storm clouds shifting aside to reveal the sun. The powerful pattern of bridges taught me to slow down and open my heart to receive the messages being sent.

Within the pattern of bridges, I found a pearl: *Love is the bridge. It is how we cross over from grief to grace. Steve, Rogers, and I are now a family of three, yet in Leanna's physical absence, we are joined by the bridge of love.*

———

In the next weeks and months, following my epiphany at the kitchen counter, new gifts of grace appeared and filled my grieving heart. I began to take a broader view, to look beyond the misery of the moment and search for the bigger picture. I started to believe that every terror, every tragedy has within it the seeds of some purpose by asking questions, such as *Why do young people have to die?* Perhaps it's because their passing makes a larger sound, takes a deeper toll, leaves a greater void, and requires those who love them to do work they probably never would have done otherwise. I began to realize that all over the world, death at an early age prompts good works from those who survive and, as a result of their grief, become determined that the child who passed will have a meaningful legacy. These instances create a ripple of service to others.

Nearly a year after her death, I made a moving discovery. While searching through Leanna's room for a book she'd recommended to me on apartheid, I found one of her journals tucked in the drawer of her nightstand. Immediately, I began to flip through the pages. My eyes fell on an entry Leanna wrote six months after our return from Africa, the trip we'd taken as a family the previous summer. Before she became ill.

The past few days I've been thinking about what I need to do to get colleges to accept me. . . . On Cappex, there was a list of some crazy things like discover a comet and name it after yourself. Obviously, I can't do that. Another one was to start your own business. And I thought: Hmm . . . maybe I can sell T-shirts that I could make and send the money to a charity.

But then it hit me. I want to volunteer in Africa. . . . I seriously think this may be a calling for me. I've never been so sure of something in my whole life. . . . I don't ever want to forget this moment. . . . I'd probably go to an orphanage or a school or something. I could give all the money to them. . . . I really want to go. Mom isn't home at the moment, so I can't tell her all this . . . I went online a 'little while ago and found quite a few places where I could go to Africa and volunteer with . . . I'm freaking out right now. . . . If you can't already tell, this is a really big deal...I've literally never felt this way before . . .xoxo

Tears filled my eyes as my daughter finally shared with me *her* epiphany. I knew at the time she had been deeply moved by the dire need she saw in Africa, but it was more than that. Leanna really wanted to go back and, this time, not as a tourist but as a helper. Finding her words then was divine timing; it was Leanna spotlighting once again that she wanted service to be a part of her legacy.

Finally, I was beginning to accept what I could not change. I had first fought that acceptance, believing it would be disrespectful to Leanna or somehow take her farther away from me. But when I finally let go of my resistance to what was, only then did I truly begin to heal. My suffering had not ended, but I was learning to honor my pain—to respect its violent power and, with Leanna as my inspiration, to find new meaning in serving others who were also in pain.

Thinking back on how I was somehow compelled to reach out to that other family just six weeks after Leanna's death, I believe that God was already whispering in my ear, offering a hint toward the burning question I had asked years before Leanna died: *Why am I here?*

Chapter 20

Life by the ocean is nourished by the eternal rhythms of the sea. Though death is a part of life's rhythm, grief itself feels land-locked and confining. Again and again, in my anguish, I found myself seeking the ocean.

In June 2013, nearly a year had passed since Leanna died. In some ways, it felt like we had just lost her, and in other ways, the journey felt like an eternity. By that time, I knew enough about my grieving to trust my instincts and not ask why, so when I felt the call to return home to Virginia Beach, I listened.

For five days, a tiny old beach cottage served as my place of escape. A three-minute walk from the Atlantic Ocean, the house provided a quiet space to rest and reflect.

The first night, after a dinner for one, I grabbed a beach chair and hauled it across the long, down-sloping wooden walkway, over the grassy dunes, and to the beach. I sat alone at the water's edge, grateful for that feeling and familiarity of home. Brushed with gentle winds in my face, I watched as the glow from the setting sun turned the white puffy clouds to pink while a sliver of the moon hung in contrast to the darkening sky.

That week, I smelled the ocean, felt the warm sand beneath my feet, and the sea salt on my skin. Sandcrabs scurried about, emerging from then disappearing into this hole and that. Ocean waves beat steadily on the shore.

One day, two carefree girls, about ten years old, were digging up sand crabs, giggling and squealing as the crabs squirmed in their hands. From behind my sunglasses, I watched and wept, remembering the times when Leanna and Rogers were around that age and we brought them to see their cousins. I looked toward the waves breaking before me and could still see my children learning to boogie board, their eyes wide with excitement as the crest of a wave brought them to shore.

The next day, as I lay sunbathing on the beach, I felt the tiny prickles of a fly landing on my arm and swatted it away. It was only then that I realized it was not a fly, after all, but a harmless little ladybug. I reached where it had tumbled upside down into the sand to gently rescue it. "I'm so sorry," I said as I set it on my towel. "Ladybugs are my favorite insect." I sat and watched its little wings flutter, eventually taking flight. *I should praise butterflies and dragonflies, too,* I thought. *They're all my favorites, really.*

And at that moment, even before my mind finished the thought, a brilliant yellow butterfly appeared, followed by a large-winged dragonfly. The pair hovered, dove, then circled me. I stared; my mouth gaped open. Not only had I never seen a butterfly or a dragonfly at Virginia Beach, but I'd also never seen a ladybug, butterfly, and dragonfly all in the same minute at any other time in my life. It was a clear sign that magic was in the air.

———

Storms rolled through, but I felt sheltered and safe. Every day, I rose before dawn, as I often had as a teenager, to witness the sunrise over the ocean. Fourteen hours later, I would watch the sun drop behind the dunes.

One morning, I walked the entire boardwalk—all fifty blocks of Virginia Beach. On no particular clock, I was outside of time, looking on as kids pedaled up and down the boardwalk on their bicycles. People perched on their hotel balconies; colorful towels draped over the railings. Seagulls swooping overhead and plodding on the sand, their feathers rippling in the wind. Families on the beach setting up chairs and umbrellas. Mothers slathering sunscreen on their children.

Out in the ocean, surfers straddled their boards, legs dangling in the water, waiting for a big wave. As I reached the end of the boardwalk, I paused at a lookout where three benches formed a sitting area. I shifted back and forth from one foot to the next then did some gentle stretches before turning back to look out toward the surfers. The sun was blinding, bouncing off the water.

As I was idling, looking toward the horizon, I spied a distinct movement and lots of splashing. I waited, straining for the next appearance. A second later, I saw it again—a dorsal fin curving out of the water then ducking back under. Then another and another. An entire pod of dolphins.

My mind's eye filled with images of Leanna's childhood drawings of dolphins dancing in the sea.

"Is that you, Leanna?" I whispered aloud, warm tears streaming down my cheeks. "Is that you?"

Yes, Mamma. Her voice was so clear, it was as if she was standing right next to me, whispering back into my ear. *I'm with you always.*

"I love you, sweet girl. Forever and ever," I cried. "You'll always be my angel."

I know, Mamma. I know. I love you too. She said, *Love will be the bridge that joins us forever and ever.*

———

When had I packed for the trip, I tossed a skirt into my suitcase, just in case. I wasn't sure if I would feel like going to church, but as Sunday rolled around, something beckoned me to go. Yet in some odd confusion, I'd meant to attend First Presbyterian but ended up among the Methodists.

As the pastor began his sermon, I swallowed hard when I realized God was trying to speak to me. The pastor was preaching on Mark 5, verses 21–43, the same sermon about two miracles of healing by Jesus, including one of a young girl.

Why has God led me here? I wondered. *What did I miss the first time?*

According to the Scripture, everyone in the town had thought the girl was gone. Everyone except for Jesus, who brought her back from the dead.

What did God want me to know? I had no clue.

What I did know was that during those five days at the beach, Leanna was everywhere. In the sunshine. In the sea air. In the waves as they rolled up on the beach. She was dancing with the dolphins and in every sunrise and sunset. Heaven and earth became one. As the boundaries outside me blurred, something inside me became clear—I was no longer separate from Leanna or God. They were all around me, and they *were* me. The veil had lifted. My seed had cracked. I had begun to move through the darkness.

———

On my final evening, I stood in the kitchen washing dishes, and a drizzling rain came to a slow drip like the last drops of water in a faucet after you turn off the shower. A heavy summer storm had just moved through, but now the sun was peeking out.

Hey! A voice inside me urged. *Go outside. Go down to the beach. Hurry!*

I grabbed a hoodie and trudged down the expanse of soaked sand to the edge of the water. To the east, the skies were dark as the storm continued its path. When I looked to the right, I had to squint at first, but I started to see faint shades of color: red . . . orange . . . yellow . . . green.

For the first time in my life, a rainbow formed right before my eyes, and Leanna's parting gift soon spread wide across the sky and over the ocean.

I nearly fell to my knees.

Chapter 21

My cell phone rang.

"Hello?"

"Hi, Beth. It's your dad," he said in a solemn tone.

"Is everything okay? You sound kind of down."

"Everything is not okay. That's the reason for my call. I was diagnosed with cirrhosis of the liver." He paused. "Beth, it's pretty far along, and I have decided to refuse treatment."

I was silent.

"Beth?"

"Yes, Dad, I'm here." My eyes filled with tears. "I don't really know what to say. I'm so sorry," I said, searching for whatever words I could to break the awkward silence. "Do you have any sense of how much longer?" I asked.

"I don't expect to make it till the end of the year. They said maybe three to six months," he replied.

———

A few weeks following my solo visit to the beach, I was back in Virginia, along with Steve and Rogers, for one last chance to be with my father. This time in Norfolk, we stayed at a hotel near Dad's apartment. Along with my three siblings, we took turns sitting by Dad's bedside as he lay with his head propped on a feather pillow, dozing off and on, rising mainly to eat.

To keep busy and try to be useful, Steve and I shopped for and prepared two of Dad's favorite meals—fish stew and chicken and dumplings. Appearing thin and frail, his body was shutting down. Thanks to hospice care, Dad was kept reasonably comfortable.

This man who had spent his entire life scrambling up the corporate ladder and building a status of power was now relying on others to care for him. For so long, he had been intent on acquiring new things. Now, he was trying to give it all away. "Beth, I want you to have those," he said, pointing toward two of his treasured abstract paintings. To others in the family, he offered photographs, clothes, shoes—everything.

I still struggled, thinking this was all too little, too late, but I was grateful to see Dad finally release his ego and be humble in the end. I believe it was a sign of his soul's progress. To be surrounded by his children in a place of love, his life finally had found meaning. After chasing illusions, this was real.

———

One day, during this last visit, as I sat by Dad's bedside, he held out a small, handsome cedar box nine inches long and four inches high. It was one I knew well. "I want you to have this," he said. When he was a young man, he had worked at a men's clothing store called The Center Shops; that's where he acquired the box. Now, in this quiet room where we expected he would draw his last breath, my dad and I looked together at the treasures he had chosen to keep in that special box: his twenty-two-karat tie pin, a pin from the time he was chair of Norfolk's Azalea

Festival, an assortment of pens engraved with his name, and a photo of his four kids with our mom, taken just after they separated. Beneath some other objects was a note, and I reached for it.

"What's this?" I asked, even though I recognized it immediately.

"How come it took you so long to come back with my form?" The letter, written in a bubbly girl's handwriting I recognize as my own, instantly delivers me to the summer of 1974.

I was ten years old, and the long days of summer felt endless as I anticipated my first-ever sojourn alone. I was off to Christian camp at the Triple-R Ranch in Chesapeake, just a forty-minute drive from home.

———

Always in a hurry, Dad drives me there at his usual breakneck speed. When we arrive, the staff collects registration paperwork. Instantly, my heart sinks as I realize that I've left mine at home. The staff informs me that without the paperwork, there are certain activities I will not be cleared for. Dad's face registers annoyance, and I'm terrified to ask but have no choice.

Frantically, I turn to him. "The form is at home on the kitchen counter!"

He looks at me in silence, but his face screams a message that this mistake is mine to own. I become sick with the shame of being so careless, as the silence hangs in the air.

"Okay, okay," he says. "I'll go get it. I'll be back."

Hours pass. Dad never could stand to be told what to do, and his rebellion blares at me, even though he left in silence: he's going to make me wait. The minutes slog along like they're wading in a marsh, and I am embarrassed and afraid the camp director will send me home.

As I wait for Dad, I watch the director file the paperwork of other campers, occasionally glancing at the clock on the wall, then back to me, then back to her forms. I sink in my chair as I imagine my father lollygagging along the roads to stretch the time.

Dad finally arrives. Complaining about the traffic, he hands me the form. Holding back the tears that threaten to embarrass me further, I swallow against the lump in my throat and mutter, "Thanks, Dad."

I pick up my duffel bag and sleeping bag and hurry to my cabin. The next evening, after the activities are over for the day, I retreat from the campfire to my bunk. Full of youthful indignation, I sit down and write Dad a letter. The cute, cartoonish pink owl on my stationery is a stark contrast to my scathing commentary. "How come it took you so long to come back with my form?" I admonish. But in the end, I retire my iron fist and before I mail the letter, I scribble a sentence at the end: "I love you, and I always will."

———

I read these last, loving words and gently replaced the letter among the other cherished contents.

I had a parting gift for Dad too—a large prayer shawl knitted with blue-gray yarn, crocheted by the same group of women from our church who had made Leanna's shawl. It was one possession he did not part with.

"Dad, don't be afraid of death," I said, looking down at him as he rested, the prayer shawl covering his large frame. "Leanna will show you the way."

He offered a soft smile and nodded.

"But I want you to do something for me, okay? Think of it as your homework. When you and Leanna find one another—when you're united—please send me a sign. Make it unmistakable so I'll know for sure."

Dad's smile went crooked as tears collected at the corners of his eyes. "I'll do my best," he said.

As Steve, Rogers, and I said our final goodbyes, Dad reached out to shake Steve's hand. "Take care of her, Steve."

Steve nodded. "I will."

I laid my hand on my father's. "I love you, Dad."

"I love you too," he replied. "All of you."

Chapter 22

Soon after Leanna passed, we received a lovely letter from Dave Varty and his wife, Shan, from the Londolozi Private Game Reserve—the reserve in South Africa where our family had such a magical time and where Leanna had vowed to return on her honeymoon.

"Steve," I said, handing him the letter. "Look at this. I can't believe it."

I watched him read, his eyebrows raising slightly. "Wow, that's so kind."

After expressing their condolences, Dave and Shan offered to memorialize Leanna on their property and make her a permanent part of the Londolozi family. They invited us to reach back to them after we had time to think about it. Several months later, the Klaubers, who had led our first trip to South Africa, invited us to join them on a return trip. It was time for us—and Leanna—to return to Londolozi.

Central to our plan for an appropriate ceremony was to take along a small urn of Leanna's ashes. As the trip approached, I phoned the airline to find out what their policy was for traveling with a person's ashes. The woman on the other end of the line was not encouraging. "I'm afraid we have restrictions on flying with human ashes. For one, they have to be removed from any metal container." My heart slumped. I didn't want to

202 | Beyond the Rainbow

think about taking Leanna's ashes out of the metal urn, so in the end, I just dropped the issue.

———

A week after visiting my father, we boarded the first plane on our journey to South Africa. We were excited about another adventure, but sorrow sat as our silent companion. Our precious girl was not with us.

"Mom?" Rogers turned to me shortly after takeoff.

"Yessir?"

"Um . . ." he shifted in his seat. "I think I broke the law."

I stiffened. "What? What do you mean?"

"Um . . . I kind of . . . I brought my little urn of Leanna's ashes," he said, breaking into a grin.

Acting entirely on his own, without a word to Steve or me, Rogers had slipped the tiny urn into the side pocket of his camera bag.

"For real? What if security had found them?"

He shrugged. "I figured I would break down in tears. You know—make a scene."

No wonder he was pacing and biting his nails when the TSA agents sent his camera bag through the machine for a second scan. Finally, though, they waved him on. Strangely, no one bothered to check the side pocket.

A smile stretched across my face. I couldn't help but feel that this was the work of an angel—one who had stepped in to help her brother carry out a plan to get her back to Africa.

———

Not long after we arrived—exhausted—at the first of two private game reserves in South Africa, I received a text from my sister Tracy.

You may want to call Dad. The end is near.

I had wanted to see Dad again after our return, but it seemed he wouldn't live that long.

Cell phone service back to the States was shaky, and I wasn't sure what to say. Walking in anxious circles on the deck of our lodge, I dialed the number. After two rings, the call dropped.

Right away, my brother Barry called me back. "Hi, Beth. Dad is asleep, but I'll wake him up so you can talk to him."

"Okay," I said, my hands shaking.

A few minutes later, I heard a faint voice. "Hello?"

"Hi, Dad. We've arrived safely in Africa and guess what? Today, we saw an amazing elephant herd, including a four-week-old baby! And then, when the sky got dark, I saw the Southern Cross, and I started praying for you, Dad." I paused then added, "I love you."

"I know," he said, whispering his very last words to me.

Barry returned to the phone. "I'll keep you updated. Ya'll be safe!"

That night, I dreamed Dad had passed. Waking the next morning, I received a text that confirmed it. Dad died five hours after our call. The hospice workers came and with compassion, took his body and, in its place, left a fresh red rose on the pillow.

The next day, as we rode around on our safari game drives, nearly all of the animals we saw were in pairs. There were two male cheetahs on a mound, searching for prey. A pair of lionesses resting in the golden grass. Two Scops owls perched in a tree. And two cheetah cubs frolicking near their mother.

That night after dinner, on the drive back to our rooms in open-air jeeps, we gazed up into the night sky. Suddenly, a break appeared in the clouds and two brilliant stars shone through.

"Dad!" I gasped, knowing at that moment, he had completed his homework. He had found Leanna. All day, he'd been trying to show me, and there, at last, I got it.

Sorry, Dad, that it took me all day to get your message. I'm so happy you and Leanna are together. Rest now in sweet peace.

Chapter 23

Finally, with excited but unsettled hearts, we boarded a prop plane for Londolozi. As it banked on its final approach to the simple airstrip carved out of the bush, Steve, Rogers, and I strained to catch a glimpse out the small window. Sure enough, the Londolozi Land Rovers were lined up along the shoulder of the runway with the rangers and trackers assembled in the shade, awaiting our arrival.

Two years had passed since we'd been there with Leanna. Would we feel the same awe and reverence for nature we had felt on our first trip? Or would we feel more sorrow and pain than comfort to be in that sacred sanctuary without her?

As soon as we stepped off the plane, our former guide, James, greeted us with a "Welcome back!" punctuated by a huge bear hug. We all piled into the Land Rovers and puttered along the dirt roads to that familiar sound of the diesel engine. *Ahhhh, We're back!!*

After dropping off our duffel bags and grabbing a quick snack in our room, we climbed back into one of the Land Rovers and ventured out for an afternoon game drive. Overhead, the blue skies disappeared as filmy gray clouds crowded out the sun. Swirling winds echoed the uncertain color of our mood. As we pulled away from camp, I wondered what animals might appear around the next turn. Leopards? Lions? Was Leanna with us, and if so, would she send us a sign?

The birds were especially active that day, with eagles and vultures swooping in the distance, buffeted by a gusty wind. Following the signals of our expert tracker, James steered us into a small clearing surrounded on three sides by a thicket of scraggly shrubs. There, lying on her belly in the yellow-brown grass, was a regal lioness. These huge cats spend most of their afternoons lounging and sleeping, saving their energy for night hunting. This lioness, however, was highly alert. Two other lionesses were nearby. One—a "sub-adult" who looked thin and a bit scruffy—hunched behind a nearby shrub. Suddenly, an enormous male sauntered into view.

After some tussling between the lion and the first lioness, James whispered that the pair was engaged in foreplay and might mate very soon. Not twenty feet from the jeep, we witnessed their amorous encounter, our eyes wide with astonishment. Their mating complete, the male, still restless, fixed his gaze on the sub-adult, hissed at her, and started toward her.

Mature lions have huge jaws, mighty teeth, and a frightening blend of size, strength, and quickness. The two cats began to fight, but the sub-adult was clearly outmatched. There was no way she could win. Yet as we held our breath, she mustered the will to fight back. Hard. Somewhere deep inside me, I knew Leanna hovered above us, cheering on the lioness.

The male, surprised by the young cat's strength and will, began to back away. Simultaneously, two mature lionesses leaped to the aid of the younger female.

"Those are her mother and aunt," James explained. One lioness cuffed the mean-spirited male and scolded him with a sudden growl, to which he replied with a full-throated roar. Three other males lying nearby moved in to see what the commotion was about. "And those are his brothers," James added. The mother of the sub-adult began to roar.

Within moments, the fight was on. Back and forth the males chased the females across the shallow Sand River. We watched as lions disappeared, then popped up in the distant reed beds, then disappeared again, only to be splashing through the river a few seconds later. The lionesses flew in and out of the thicket, trying to distract the males and divert them from the weakened youngster. In all the roaring and dust, James tried to maneuver our jeep to give us a better vantage point. But the animals were moving far too quickly, so we sat still and let the drama unfold around us.

In this swirl of activity, my mind was swirling too. *Leanna, are you seeing all of this? Or better yet, are you causing all of this?* The wind kicked up, its whirring filling first my ears, then my head, then my heart. And I knew.

On our ride back to camp that evening, we couldn't stop talking about the wildlife show we'd seen on our very first game drive since returning to Londolozi. The spectacle even featured some exceptional female strength and bravery. Later in the week, we were pleased to learn that the three lionesses had been spotted by another group of visitors, who said the youngster had likely eaten well, as her behavior was livelier.

Although we were new at looking for Leanna's signs, none of us doubted that she had stirred the pot that afternoon, making her presence known.

———

The following morning broke cool and cloudy. After our first game drive of the day was over and we enjoyed breakfast in the main lodge of the camp, Shan and Dave asked to meet with me, Steve, Michael, and Terri. We convened outside at a private picnic table sheltered by a thatched roof.

Months before, when we had received the letter from Dave and Shan, the idea of honoring Leanna at Londolozi didn't seem quite real. Now, with all of us assembled at the table, the deep emotion within me began to rise to the surface. I took a deep breath, filling my lungs with the cool South African air. Steve reached for my hand.

Once huddled around the picnic table, Shan looked us lovingly in the eyes and uttered these words, forever ingrained in my heart: "We'd like to offer three ideas for you to think about to memorialize your beautiful daughter. All are congruent with nature. You can choose to do all three; or you can do two, one, or none at all. It's completely up to you."

"First of all," Shan continued, "we can plant a Kigelia tree in the small village at Londolozi."

Oh, yeah, I thought to myself. *We have a photo of Leanna and the other kids climbing this massive tree, with Rogers perched higher than any of them.*

"By planting the tree in the village, it will be protected from the elephants and cared for by our staff. Second, we can build a cairn—a small stone monument—at the base of a wild fig tree at Ximpalapala Koppie. The cairn would be a safe, protected place for the small urn of ashes you brought from home. If you decide to go with this idea, we will bring enough rocks to the area for us all to build it. And third, we can climb to the top of Ximpalapala to watch the sunset after the cairn is built. There, we can spend some reflective time together. These are the three ideas we can offer you."

By the time Shan finished, all of us were crying. Finally, I gathered myself. "We are so moved by your loving gesture to our family. Thank you." I looked at Steve and his quiet nod said, *Whatever you think.* I turned back to Shan. "I don't want to sound greedy, but I'm in favor of all three." Everyone else smiled and nodded in agreement, our cheeks glistening with tears.

"Wonderful!" Shan replied. "We will schedule this on the third afternoon of your stay to give us time to get everything set up for you."

As Steve and I started to get up from the table to collect our thoughts and try to absorb all of this, Michael piped in. "Wait, before you go, there's one more thing we want to talk to you about. Terri and I have been thinking of other ways to honor Leanna, and we have come up with an idea."

Unbeknownst to us, Terri and Michael had been thinking of honoring Leanna by setting up a special fund tied to the Good Work Foundation—a South African organization that offers digital education to school-aged kids in rural parts of their country. Considering Leanna's desire to help African kids, it seemed like a perfect fit. They wanted to present the idea to us at the meeting but were nervous that they didn't yet have a name for the fund.

"On the game drive this morning, I prayed to Leanna," Terri explained. "I told her: 'Leanna, we need a little help with a name for this fund in your honor so we can raise money for South African kids who really need it. Can you send us a sign, please?'"

A few minutes later, they came upon two leopards—a mother and daughter who were hissing at each other. The leopards soon resolved their little conflict and lay down in the grass, flicking their tails in the air. "And then, I kid you not," Terri said, "in the next second, their two tails came together in the shape of a heart." Later, Terri would show me evidence of the incredible sight on her camera. "I said to Michael, 'Well, that was sure an all-heart moment! Let's name it the All Heart Fund!'" They headed back to camp, knowing Leanna had given them the sign they needed.

"We thought we could set up a fund in her honor and tie it to the Good Work Foundation as a fundraising auxiliary. What do you think?"

It was too much to bear. "Of course!" I cried. "I love it! Let's talk more about it in the next few days."

We all rose from the table, hugged one another, and wiped our faces. Steve and I collected our things from the main lodge and walked in silence to our rooms for a short rest before the afternoon game drive.

———

The third day of the trip arrived quickly. As I had experienced so often since Leanna's passing, the love and gratitude I felt were mixed with sadness and pain.

Just before 3:00 p.m., Steve, Rogers, and I walked down to the small village where the Vartys and the Klaubers, along with the trackers and guides, were waiting. The mood was somber.

The sky was brushed with wispy clouds; the foliage fluttered in the cool breeze. About twenty of us stood around with our hands folded. Two trees—a sapling and a larger tree—stood before us, ready to be planted in their pre-dug holes. Silently, Steve stepped forward and gently tossed into the moist, black dirt a handwritten letter to Leanna. He and Rogers then knelt and placed dirt around the roots of the sapling while the others lovingly planted the second tree. We took photos, stood silent for several long moments, then climbed into our Land Rover. From there, our mournful procession headed toward Ximpalapala.

When we arrived, everyone climbed out of the vehicles and walked quietly to the site of the old fig tree that sat in a shaded area at the base of the mountain. I was grateful for the rangers that stood watch, as this area was popular for leopards and their cubs. The roots of the fig tree stretched like long fingers toward the earth, wrapping down around a large boulder. On the ground next to the tree was a pile of rocks that Shan and Dave had gathered for the cairn. We huddled together beneath the ancient fig, and I read aloud the passage from Leanna's diary about devoting her life to mission work in Africa.

As I concluded, there was a flash of green overhead. We looked skyward as three brilliant emerald-colored pigeons flew overhead. In my mind, I heard a voice. *Beginning, middle, and end. Water, heaven, and earth. Body, soul, and spirit.*

Rogers, Steve, and I began to pick up the rocks. Together, we built the base for the cairn. Then, Rogers took the small urn of his sister's ashes, along with his angel wing bracelet from the hospital, and placed them inside the rocks. Then, the rest of the group came forward and, one by one, placed their rocks on top of ours. When the small but sturdy monument was completed, Steve placed a hand on the top of the cairn and prayed a silent prayer.

Still in silence, we all hiked nearly four stories to the top of the koppie and gathered on granite boulders for the final part of our memorial. We each found a private spot and watched as God painted the sky with streaks of fiery reds and brilliant oranges. When the sun approached the horizon and took on a deep red hue, Shan pulled out her iPad and played a song she had chosen for this moment called, "Long Time Sun." This melodic song sealed our spiritual connection with each other and our beloved Leanna, on the land she'd vowed to return to.

While Steve and I sat on a large boulder with our legs dangling over the edge, a friend took a photo of us from behind as we watched the sun disappear. Later, when we saw the image, my skin erupted in goosebumps as I noticed a beam of light shining over my right shoulder—a lightsaber, straight from heaven.

Leanna had returned to Africa, after all, with the help of her brother.

Chapter 24

"Mom, there's no way I can miss work camp this year. I know I'll feel better in a few days," Leanna pleads, her hands pressed together in prayer just below her chin. "Please, Mom?"

"Okay, sweetheart. I have my reservations, but the doctor says it's okay. You MUST obey his orders. Get lots of rest," I remind her.

"I will, Mom. I promise."

———

The first time Leanna traveled to West Virginia for a mission trip was in 2011. She joined 120 other teens at the Cabell-Lincoln work camp where the true meaning of service nourished her soul. That feeling of oneness beckoned, and she vowed to return the following year.

The unspeakable tragedy that cut her second trip short never left my soul. When Leanna's life on earth ended in 2012, I made it my mission to join the work crews each year, go to the place where she gave her final gift to this world, and keep alive what she started.

The camp was born fifty-plus years ago out of faith that a team of Christian volunteers could do worthy work, repairing old churches and the ramshackle homes of the poor. Homeowners from Cabell County and Lincoln County, West Virginia apply for repairs, with about thirty receiving help each year. A board of directors, led by The Reverend Rick Wilson, ranks the homes based on need, and in the summer, high-school students from six states and a handful of adults, including crew leaders fully adept in construction, ride in Greyhound buses to the hills of West Virginia. With paintbrushes and caulk guns, circular saws and sandpaper, their crews repair roofs, replace siding, or build a little girl or boy the first bedroom they've ever had. Always, there is the smell of sawdust and the shimmering, sweltering heat. Dirty and sweaty, I join them to push through our exhaustion for that feeling of pride and satisfaction in a job well done.

In life, so much of the time we dwell on the past or worry about the future; we are separated by our region, level of income, and our spiritual and other beliefs. At the camp in West Virginia, those divisions vanish. Volunteers, crew leaders, residents—all of us are one and the same. Together, we spend an entire week living in the moment, helping others, finding fellowship, and feeling unity and the presence of God. For so much of my life, I had yearned for that yet rarely found it—a place where everyone is treated with respect and accepted just as they are. People drop their guard and allow themselves to be loved, even by those they've only recently met.

During Leanna's final visit to the work camp in 2012, she was assigned to the home of a young single mother named Angel and her two young boys, Brody and Kyle. When Leanna's team arrived, they could see the ground beneath the house through large cracks in the flooring. The walls had gaping holes, and much of the porch roofing was caving in. The work crew did all they could in five days to make the home warm, safe, and dry. Most of the crew, at least. Listless, nauseated, and short of breath, Leanna remained in the church van, but before she flew home, she mustered the strength to meet Angel and her children.

Less than four weeks later, Leanna was gone from this world. Angel learned of her death when Rick Wilson paid her a visit one day in late July. A year later, he told me that Angel and the crew had decided to dedicate her home to Leanna's memory.

In the summer of 2013, Steve and I flew to West Virginia for the first time and drove to the camp's home base at Asbury Woods. Rick met us and drove us to Angel's home, nearly an hour away. As the miles passed, the roads transitioned from smoothly paved two-lane state highways to patchy, older county roads, then to gravel surfaces, and finally, to winding dirt roads, full of potholes.

These were the humble, winding roads that had led Leanna to her last work on earth, in a state hundreds of miles from home. I wanted to know them because they were some of the last roads she had traveled. As we bumped and jostled our way toward Angel's house, I imagined how Leanna's stomach must have churned on that last rocky road. Yet she never complained. I thought, too, of all the roads I had traveled—and would continue to travel—because of Leanna's life.

When we finally pulled up to Angel's house, I was aghast at the sight before me—a decrepit wooden structure hardly habitable. Angel stood on the porch, her eyes squinting from the afternoon sun; the work crew waved from the roof. Propped against the house was a wooden ladder built on-site by the crew leader with "Leanna Knopik House" painted on its rungs. Walking through the house, it was obvious that many of the repairs were mere Band-Aids; this old house was not structurally sound.

"How do people live in these conditions? Why is Angel's house in such bad shape?" I asked Rick later as we drove back to the camp.

"It's a family home, passed down from one generation to the next, and most recently to Angel," Rick replied. "She's expected to keep it in the family and, eventually, pass it on, as well. Poverty has a tenacious hold on these families," he explained, "and real change is hard to make. But hopefully, these repairs will see Angel and her kids through the next winter."

After a long day of work, each crew returned to base camp, showered, then met at the mess hall for a buffet dinner. Afterward, down at the pavilion, with picnic tables all around and in the presence of students and leaders, we held an evening worship service in Leanna's honor. There were special pink t-shirts with the Romans 12:2 verse printed on the back, songs, and personal tributes where people shared their memories of Leanna.

Rick Wilson invited us to speak at the service, and in anticipation, Steve and I had brought with us Leanna's work clothes from 2011—her tennis shoes and some jeans speckled with paint. When it was our turn, Steve held up Leanna's shoes and said, "This is where Leanna spent her last days—in mission, in service to others."

Of the countless tears I have shed since Leanna's illness and death, that night was the hardest I have ever cried. We all cried together. There in West Virginia, in the place that captured my daughter's heart, my own broken heart spilled over with love. I felt at one with Leanna, with the kids, with the crew leaders, and with God. These people had only been with Leanna for five days, yet because of the fellowship and hard work they shared, they truly *knew* her. As I looked out over the tear-filled eyes all around me, I thought, *It's not how long we're here on earth that matters, but rather, how deeply we commit ourselves to the work we are called to do in the time that we have.*

We had all signed wish lanterns made of tissue-thin paper, and at the very end of the service, some of the kids in the Florida group released the lanterns, along with their prayers, to float out over the vast green lawn as we all gathered in a large circle holding hands. The heat from the tiny fires inside the lanterns lifted them up, up. Steve and I watched their bright lights rise into the night sky as a few of the kids played a guitar rendition of "Fix You."

———

That fertile field at Asbury Woods is in a sort of natural bowl. The kids throw frisbees and footballs there. On the two sides of this grassy bowl, one hundred yards apart, stand two stately clusters of Australian pines. The camp's board of directors used some of the money donated in Leanna's honor to have two stone benches made, and one now sits beneath each cluster of pines, facing the other across the field.

Into each bench is carved Romans 12:2, the Bible verse Leanna had painstakingly painted onto that bright pink t-shirt:

> *Do not be conformed to this world, but continually be transformed by the renewal of your minds so that you may be able to determine what God's will is—what is proper, praising and perfect.*

When I first saw the benches, the inscription at the top read: "In Loving Tribute to Leanna Mae Knopic." They had misspelled our last name (and would later fix it). Leanna always thought it was funny that people couldn't spell "Knopik," so I smiled when I saw it. It felt like one of her little jokes.

The next morning, Steve and I left West Virginia and returned home enriched yet with heavy hearts. Martha Beck once wrote, "Feel the way both grief and love move in your heart and how they form a deep sense of connection that is resonant with truth." I suppose I will live with that dichotomy for the rest of my life. As long as I am here on earth, my heart will overflow with both love and pain.

———

In the same way that Leanna's story continues to unfold, there is more to the story of Angel and the house that was named in Leanna's honor. That same year, around two months after having traveled to West Virginia, Steve and I were dining in a local Italian restaurant when I received a horrifying text from Rick. It was a series of photos of Angel's home burnt to the ground, the ashes still smoldering.

Staring out the window, I felt numb. *What does this mean?*

Fortunately, the family was safe, though tragically they lost their dogs in the fire. After a brief pause to process the shock, Steve and I shifted into gear and started raising money to buy the family a used mobile home. Members of our church pitched in, and we managed to exceed our goal of $20,000. It took a few months to collect the funds, buy the mobile home, and deliver it to the remote area. In the interim, Angel moved in with her mother, but through God's grace, they were relieved of the burden that was literally rotting out from under them. This was yet another miracle that grew out of Leanna's life and death.

One year later, on a bright day in June, I took my second trip to West Virginia, this time with my sister, Tracy. In her white SUV with the radio playing in the background, we drove out Highway 64 from Richmond, admiring the mountains and talking about Tracy's kids and the feel of an empty nest. Finally, we arrived at our hotel in Huntington, West Virginia, downed a quick dinner, then drove to camp, rushing to make the evening worship service.

Within minutes, the songs began, raucous and joyous. People who came here every year were rejoicing in their return to this magical place. As the service ended and the sun began to set, Rick pulled me to the side.

"Beth, I'd love if you would agree to be part of the worship service tomorrow. Our theme is 'Love Works' as you know, and I thought maybe you could share your story with the group."

I felt my breath catch. "I um . . . sure, I'll think about it."

I hadn't come to West Virginia prepared to make a speech. Part of me wanted to tell Rick that I didn't think I was up for it. By this time, though, God and I had been through so much together a voice inside me said, *Let God decide.*

The next morning, Tracy and I drove to see a second home that had been dedicated to Leanna. After leaving there, I phoned Bob, a board member who had offered to drive us to Angel's "new" trailer home. I was so excited to see Angel and the boys, along with the home we'd secured for them.

During the hour-long drive to Angel's house, I felt Leanna's presence so intensely that if she was any closer to me, she would have been sitting in my lap. Bob is a gentle soul who once ran the camp. With his light-blue button-down shirt and his gray hair, wire-rimmed glasses, and warm Kentucky accent, I found myself opening up to him about the turns that my spiritual journey had taken since Leanna had passed.

"When Leanna died, I stopped talking to God for a while," I said. "We had so many people praying for Leanna, and I had been so dedicated to God all of my life; I couldn't imagine why he abandoned us that way."

"And now?" Bob asked.

"Now, I feel like I'm beginning to grasp the meaning of Leanna's life and the purpose of her death," I said. "I suppose part of that understanding came from simply asking why and begging for answers. Leanna's passing left an enormous hole in my life and in my heart, but I have a choice about how I fill that hole. And I guess what I've discovered is that God rushes in and fills that hole with love and grace—a different kind than I've ever known before. And maybe it's a kind I wouldn't have known otherwise. For that and for so many other reasons, I can see that Leanna's death, and now her legacy, has meaning and a purpose. I don't know if any of this makes sense, Bob, but maybe I can put it a little more simply. In my desperation to understand *why* and to find meaning in my loss, God has shown me the beauty that has come from her death."

Bob was silent for a long moment, his face displaying a tender smile. "Beth," he said. "God is at work in your life."

Finally, we reached the road where Angel lived. After two quick turns, we were there. As we parked the car, I stared out the window and could see that the dilapidated house of last year was now a modern mobile home. We see God only partially, through dreams and signs, but on that West Virginia road, I saw a whole miracle, one where God's gifts and our own were joined.

Angel swayed back and forth in the doorway with one of the boys on her hip. She invited us in and offered to show us around—a small master bedroom, two bathrooms, a full kitchen, and a living room. "And here's the boys' room." We peeked in to see twin beds and stacks of clothes neatly folded.

As I handed Angel a loaf of bread I had bought at the corner market, I asked, "Is there anything that we can do for you?"

"Well, yes," she replied, accepting the bread with a smile. "I really need to find a job." Then, she glanced over at Bob. "Can you help?" she asked.

"I can certainly try," he replied.

As we lingered in the kitchen, I turned to Angel. "Tell me about the day the house burnt down. What happened?"

She looked back at me and took a deep breath. With misty eyes and a bit of a drawl, she began, "It was a Sunday morning in August. The boys and I had gone out to see my mom like we normally do. . . . And when we pulled up to the house a few hours later, everything had burnt to the ground."

"I'm so sorry," I said, reaching out to place a hand on her shoulder.

"At first, it looked like there was nothin' left but a pile of burnt wood and twisted metal," she continued. "Then, as I walked around, I found Leanna's ladder over there," she said, pointing toward her backyard shed. We followed Angel to the back door, and she opened it to show us where she kept the ladder now. "I just couldn't believe it," she whispered with goosebumps rising on her arms. I couldn't believe it, either—the ladder was completely unscathed by the fire.

By then it was late afternoon, and when the youngest, shyest boy retreated to his mother's bedroom, I knew it was time to go. We still had a long drive ahead of us. I hugged Angel and thanked her for letting us visit.

"Thank *you*," she said. "For everything."

———

Before Leanna died, I had never been much of a public speaker. I had no great skill at it and was always terrified of it, never wanting to be the center of attention in any crowd. After Leanna's passing, I felt called to join Toastmasters, but I had to force myself to attend the meetings. I should have been able to give a simple speech, but the few times I tried, I labored to write out my remarks then used them as my security blanket with my eyes glued to the paper.

That day, as we pulled away from Angel's home, my heart full, I pondered Rick's request that I share my story that evening. I had prayed on it but had not yet decided. I had no prepared remarks and no security blanket to help deliver coherent thoughts. But with the worship service just a few hours away, I found myself perfectly calm as I awaited God's direction.

At dinner, I found a seat next to Rick. "Have you decided, Beth?" he asked. I hesitated. "These kids need to hear your story."

"Okay," I heard myself say. "I'll tell my story." I figured I should at least be able to do that. God hadn't wanted me to speak at Leanna's funeral, but now he did.

After dinner, we traipsed down the hill together and gathered at the pavilion. Though preoccupied with the task before me, I also felt a strange sense of peace. I had no idea how to organize my thoughts and, at that point, my talk had no beginning, middle, or end. But I found comfort in the love of everyone in the audience, and I trusted God to provide the words.

Following the music, Rick walked up to the podium and reminded everyone of the camp's theme, "Love Works." He talked about Leanna and her work at the camp, her illness, and her passing. Then he brought me forward.

"Leanna's mother is here with us tonight, and she is going to share with you her story and how she has walked through grief these past two years. Please, let's welcome Beth Knopik," Rick said as he scanned the crowd, looking for me.

I hopped down from my perch on the concrete wall, nearly 150 people watching as I made my way to the podium. Instinctively, I took the microphone off the stand and moved closer to the audience. With all eyes fixed on me, I felt calm.

"Thank you for the opportunity to share my journey," I began. "I want to be clear—without the love and support of others, I never would be where I am today, standing in front of you with a heart filled with awe and with gratitude." Then, I waited with an open heart for God's help.

I began my story at the end of Leanna's life on earth, talking about our time in the hospital and how lost I'd felt then, living in constant fear. I explained that in those darkest of days I hadn't even known how to pray and had wondered, *Where is God, anyway?*

When I spoke to the teens and adults about feeling completely abandoned by God, I could see their eyes glisten. All the right words came to me as if on their own, and I knew this smooth transition to public speaking was God's work. It had to be.

I continued.

"At first, when Leanna died, I had no idea how to move forward. I had no hope for my future. I wouldn't say that I eventually found God again; it's just that I came to realize I had never really lost God. My entire relationship with God and my understanding of God evolved—and is still evolving—into something entirely new. In some ways, it's hard to describe, but as the dark clouds of torment and confusion began to lift, I started to experience a kind of grace I had never known before."

Often in life, I had wondered, "Why didn't God give me more confidence?" Now it was clear—because my lack of it helped me reach a broader audience. What I had perceived as a weakness was my greatest strength. Had I marched up there full of confidence, with perfectly prepared remarks, I would not have connected with those people as I did in those moments. In my imperfection, offering them nothing but my own vulnerability and sincerity, they could see themselves in me.

As I continued my talk, with all those loving eyes upon me, I felt myself getting lighter. Not metaphorically but literally lighter on my feet. Somehow my physical state was shifting as I spoke. In the way you just know things, I was aware that my intellect and my soul had aligned and were working together in perfect unison. I understand that may sound strange, but many baffling things like that, beyond the edge of reason and logic, have happened to me since Leanna passed, and I've stopped asking why.

As the story of losing my daughter brought us fully into the present moment, hearts opened, and tears flowed freely. United under that open-air pavilion where Leanna performed skits and sang songs three years before, we were one in the sacred presence of each other. When lightning bugs appeared, God's voice whispered in the breeze, "Amen."

Reflections

Leanna and I were together for sixteen brief years in the long, long history of this planet. I am honored and grateful to have had that earthly time with her, and because of her death, not only have I grown, I've also seen other people's faith grow and their souls evolve. This collective movement in consciousness, bringing others to God—or even questioning God's will—has revealed part of the bigger plan in Leanna's passing that helped to ease my pain.

Thinking back on those thirty days in the hospital, I had thought when I saw those rainbows, *Everything will be okay.* I've learned that what happened *is* okay; it's just not the way I wanted it to be. It's God's version of okay. He was saying, "Trust in me. I am with you always. My love for you is deeper than you will ever imagine and stronger than you could ever know. In time, you will see more and better understand." Precisely because the rainbows weren't what I thought they were, they led me to see that there is way more to life than what's right in front of us. The rainbows taught me to look beyond my earthly desires and open my eyes to see God's plan. They held out the promise that something good would come of this, and that promise gave me hope. I still celebrate every time I see a rainbow.

Over the years, I've learned to embrace my pain. In truth, I don't believe I will ever be pain-free because the pain helps to keep the memory of Leanna from fading. Every teardrop I shed for Leanna honors her soul and signifies the fountain of love that pours from my heart. Without love, there would be no pain. Perhaps someday, I will feel Leanna's love and presence without pain, but I'm not there yet. As I walk this path my faith continues to open, like a spring flower after a long, brutal winter.

While I accept my pain and hold it close, what I will *not* accept is endless suffering, for pain and suffering are two very different things. The debilitating despair, the acute suffering I once felt, has fallen away over the years, thank God. No one can continue to live that way. However, suffering does have its purpose in the grieving process. It brings you back to the beginning; it marks the end of the life you knew and starts another. I view it now as a stepping stone to joy and to God, even if the path seems long and arduous.

Since July 19, 2012, I've been in awe of the many blessings that have come from loss. Right after a wrenching loss, we are in too much pain to see the blessings. We stare up at the night sky and scour the heavens, searching for a gift that's right in front of us. It's too soon for us to see it.

But new perspectives and a deeper understanding of loss come with time. To reach this place, we must not rush through grief but give despair and suffering its due. Allow the river to carry us. If we avoid the pain or push it down, we cannot move forward. That was Steve's way of coping in those first months and even years, though about five years after Leanna's death, he finally did see a counselor to help him process his grief. And even that "chance" meeting had Leanna's delicate fingerprints all over it.

Steve now sees the blessings of Leanna's passing and so have others who have experienced such loss. In time, you too will see the gifts. Many of them. I don't believe tragedies happen without real meaning and purpose. These gifts are God's grace.

My gifts have come in many forms. For one, I am blessed with many new connections—all sorts of people whom I would never have known without Leanna's passing. The West Virginia work camp is one example. Having witnessed the love of everyone there, like my daughter before me, I am drawn to that feeling of oneness year after year. Along with many others, my new friends in West Virginia have taught me the true meaning of grace. I have also witnessed the power of Leanna's legacy, rippling out to hundreds of people through blood drives held in her honor and the digital learning centers in South Africa where kids in rural villages have an opportunity for a better future. When I step back to look at the beauty and impact of Leanna's life and death, my heart aches with a love so deep, I am unable to comprehend its enormity. In time, being mindful with meditation and prayer will help me to more fully grasp and absorb God's divine plan.

I work hard to take care of myself. Thanks to Valerie's sessions just after Leanna's death, I realized yoga could bring me peace and even moments of supreme joy. With practice, I found those moments of peace lasting longer and longer. And eventually, I opened to the realization that peace is *not* a separate compartment of our lives—that despite life's chaos, peace can be a constant state of being, a connection never lost.

I try to take deep cleansing breaths, exercise, eat and sleep well, and trust the sudden turns in the road. I am much more patient now—and much less thrown by the inevitable shifts in life. Trials are here to help us grow and, like yoga poses, bring us closer to a blending of mind and spirit—closer to God.

I still ground myself with my love of the natural world, just as I did in my youth. I also use prayer to stay closer to God. At one time, my prayers were careful, self-conscious, and directed at a certain person or problem. I was praying the way an amateur photographer snaps a picture: pull out the camera, point it at the subject, and click. Now, through this journey with Leanna, my praying is second nature—truthful, transparent, without thought or hesitation—while trusting God's will. In prayer as second nature lies deep peace, and only when we stop focusing on the material and start accessing our spirituality can we find it. Sometimes, wind chimes sound when there isn't the slightest breeze.

Leanna is always with me, but sometimes I feel her presence more strongly than others. On the days when I especially long for her, I put on one of her hoodies and feel her spirit, her presence, and her love. I wear Leanna's angel wing bracelet on my wrist; whenever I get too busy with life, that bracelet reminds me to breathe, slow down, and take in her spirit. The last words I ever spoke to her were, "I know you will always be with me," and that pact between us will always remain. I know without a doubt Leanna will keep her end of the deal. If I start to wander, she will send me a sign through owl calls outside my bedroom window or a Coldplay song on the radio. I also think of her whenever I see a cloud in the shape of an angel. I probably miss many of Leanna's signs—but that's okay. The more I listen, the more I hear. The more I look, the more I see.

Though my time with Leanna was fated to be brief, the memories and the love between us will last forever. When I look back on our time together, I've realized that my greatest days with Leanna weren't when I was parenting her but just being with her, caught up in a shared moment together, with no self-consciousness, no sense of how fleeting life is. Snatches of conversation, little jokes, shared moments that slip away and are gone. It brings to light how much in life we take for granted.

Thinking back on some of the mysteries from around the time of Leanna's death, I understand why God brought me multiple times to hear the sermon from the Book of Mark, Chapter Five. Just like all those blessings I had yet to see, it was hiding in plain sight. Verse 34 reads, "He said to her: 'Daughter, your faith has healed you. Go in peace and be freed from your suffering.'" Jesus healed me. My faith had wavered, but He healed me and brought me closer to grace.

I've also learned along this road that our children belong not to us but to God. Yes, as parents we have them for a few years, and we get to play with them, laugh with them, and hold them in our arms. Then they're gone, off to fulfill their own purposes, walking the path that God has planned for them.

I see now my purpose in life: to have raised my daughter and my son; to honor Leanna's legacy, and to spread it far and wide. Leanna's friend Stephanie says, "Everyone should have the chance to meet one Leanna in their life, but few people do." I want to help more people know Leanna and what her life was about—to spread her joy and her desire to help others. I want to take that entrusted baton and run with it.

Honoring Leanna's legacy by turning my pain into purpose helped heal my struggling soul. After reaching out to the family whose daughter died in a car accident, I contacted another family . . . and another. Once, I spent three hours on the phone with a grieving mom. "You *will* have peace again. Faith and trust," I told her. When reaching out to others, I might start with a text, then a phone call, and then we'll meet face-to-face. Many parents who have endured the death of a child are afraid to get involved with another such family, and understandably so. They are afraid they'll have a setback themselves. But there are many other ways to be of service, so I encourage you to find something that speaks to *your* heart.

My mother always taught me to trust the process of life, but into my late forties, I had lost sight of that trust. I was never sure I was on a path to make a difference in the world.

I now have a richer notion of success. When you are living your truth, in joy and in service, and when you are guided by your heart, your life will speak for itself. I believe a review of my life will show that I brought into the world two precious children. While Leanna's legacy ripples out into the world, Rogers is forging a meaningful path in the wake of his sister's death. He still wears a silver angel wing cuff and his green "Team Leanna" wristband every day, as does Steve. To this day, Rogers has largely kept his grief over Leanna to himself; at least, he hasn't shared it with me. Still, I imagine it's a loss he feels keenly, sometimes more than others. But I have peace knowing Leanna is with him, watching out for him, protecting him. In the audio piece he made for his sound mixing class where he described saying goodbye to Leanna, he reflected: "I don't remember the last thing she said to me. Could be she said something meaningful or beautiful, but I don't care too much because she speaks to me daily—in dragonflies, blue skies, or tears in my eyes. She's not by my side but, instead, in disguise, guiding me to the greatness of what lies ahead."

Where is she? I had asked on that terrible first night after Leanna died— when sleep seemed impossible. *Where is my daughter?* Now, I *know.* Leanna is present when I see dolphins in the blue waters of Sarasota Bay. She rides in the car with me as we blast the radio, and she sits next to me in church. Leanna is in Sarasota giving the gift of life through blood drives held in her honor, and she's in West Virginia repairing homes. She's in a cairn in a gorgeous game reserve in South Africa, near plains of golden grass that seem to go on forever, and she is in the hearts of everyone who knew her. Now that you have read our story, she is in yours too.

There's still a lot I don't understand about the death of a child, but this I do know: If we keep our eyes on the larger picture and our hearts open, we will embrace the new path before us. And no matter where you are on your grief's journey, grace *will* be revealed, and you *will* have peace and joy again.

Finally, I have realized that death is not final. Death is not death at all; it's a rebirth, a renewal, a resurrection. Love remains and grace abounds.

Recommended Reading

Finding Inner Courage,
Mark Nepo, Conari Press, 2007

A Grace Disguised, How a Soul Grows Through Loss,
Jerry Sittser, Zondervan, 1995

Proof of Heaven, A Neurosurgeon's Journey into the Afterlife,
Eben Alexander, M.D., Simon & Schuster, 2012

Dying to be Me, My Journey from Cancer, to Near Death, to True Healing,
Anita Moorjani, Hay House, 2012

The Book of Joy,
His Holiness the Dalai Lama and Archbishop Desmond Tutu, Avery, 2016

7 Lessons from Heaven, How Dying Taught Me to Live a Joy-Filled Life,
Mary C. Neal, M.D., Convergent, 2017

Lament for a Son,
Nicholas Wolterstorff, Wm. B Eerdmans Publishing Company, 1987

The Beauty of What Remains, How Our Greatest Fear Becomes Our Greatest Gift,
Steve Leder, Avery, 2021

About the Author

Beth Knopik, a Virginia native, has lived in Sarasota for most of her adult life. She has worked as a commercial banking officer, raised a family, and now gives her time to local, regional, and international non-profits. In 2012, her daughter Leanna passed away from heart disease. Leanna was sixteen.

As a certified life coach, Beth has written articles about grief, co-leads support groups for Tidewell Hospice, and offers stress management coaching for parents of children with special needs. Beth's life mission is to preserve, share, and expand Leanna's legacy, and this book is a part of that plan. Beth's husband, Steve, is retired after a long career with Bealls, Inc. Their son, Rogers, is pursuing a career in film production.

A free ebook edition is available with the purchase of this book.

To claim your free ebook edition:

1. Visit MorganJamesBOGO.com
2. Sign your name CLEARLY in the space
3. Complete the form and submit a photo of the entire copyright page
4. You or your friend can download the ebook to your preferred device

Morgan James BOGO™

A **FREE** ebook edition is available for you or a friend with the purchase of this print book.

CLEARLY SIGN YOUR NAME ABOVE

Instructions to claim your free ebook edition:
1. Visit MorganJamesBOGO.com
2. Sign your name CLEARLY in the space above
3. Complete the form and submit a photo of this entire page
4. You or your friend can download the ebook to your preferred device

Print & Digital Together Forever.

Snap a photo

Free ebook

Read anywhere

CPSIA information can be obtained
at www.ICGtesting.com
Printed in the USA
JSHW020820100922
30331JS00001B/1